THE WRITE PATH

Also by Lauren Kessler

Raising the Barre:
Big Dreams, False Starts and My Midlife Quest to
Dance The Nutcracker

Counterclockwise:
My Year of Hypnosis, Hormones, Dark Chocolate and
Other Adventures in the World of Anti-Aging

My Teenage Werewolf:
A Mother, A Daughter, A Journey Through the
Thickets of Adolescence

Dancing with Rose:
Finding Life in the Land of Alzheimer's

Clever Girl:
Elizabeth Bentley, the Spy Who Ushered in the McCarthy Era

Happy Bottom Riding Club:
The Life and Times of Pancho Barnes

Full Court Press:
A Season in the Life of a Winning Basketball Team and
the Women Who Made It

Stubborn Twig:
Three Generations in the Life of a Japanese American Family

THE WRITE PATH

Essays on the art of writing

and the joy of reading

LAUREN KESSLER

Monroe Press

2015

Cover design and illustration by Liza Mana Burns
Book design and layout by Jackson Hager

Published by Monroe Press
Eugene, OR
www.Monroe.press

ISBN: **0-9767649-4-6**

To
Richard J. Hawkey,
who told me I might some day be a writer

CONTENTS

THE ART OF WRITING

ACKNOWLEDGMENTS

I can tell you the moment I knew I wanted to be a writer. I was sitting under the crabapple tree on the front lawn of the house on Richard Lane reading *My Friend Flicka*. It was the beginning of summer vacation. I was nine years old.

And something happened.

I lost all sense of time and place – and myself. I was transported into the world of the book. I remember when my mother called me in for lunch, and it took me completely by surprise that I was sitting in front of a split-level on Long Island and not out on Goose Bar Ranch, just outside Cheyenne, Wyoming. That I was – oh right – a girl with a tabby cat as a pet, not a boy with a sorrel filly.

I knew then – although certainly my nine-year-old self would not have expressed it this way – that this is what I wanted to do. I wanted to use words to create worlds that people could lose themselves in. My career has been in nonfiction, in storytelling (or narrative) nonfiction because I am fascinated by true stories – real people, real events – and I love the immersion and the research that goes long with this kind of work.

I owe my life as a writer to Mary O'Hara (author of *My Friend Flicka*) and Marjorie Kinnan Rawlings (*The Yearling*) – yes, I was horse obsessed – and later to Raymond Chandler and Lewis Thomas, to Vladmir Nabokov and May Sarton, to Joan Didion, John McPhee, Kent Haruf (the list goes on) who created worlds for me to inhabit and allowed me to live multiple lives. I learned to write by reading (and, of course, by writing). My teachers and mentors were people I never met who didn't know I existed. I acknowledge them all.

THE JOY OF READING

1

I HEART BOOKS

These pages tell our life stories

> Outside of a dog, a book is man's best friend.
> Inside of a dog it's too dark to read.
> – Groucho Marx

Scent triggers memory in a special, direct and immediate way. This was explained to me once – some kind of hardwiring from nasal receptors to frontal lobe – but not well enough so that I can explain it now. But we all know it's true: a whiff of something, cut grass, gasoline, chocolate chip cookies, and we're transported to another time and place, an entire scene evoked, a little drama played out on the stage of the mind. I smell garlic sautéing in olive oil (which I often do, garlic being the staff of life around our house), and I see my mother in the kitchen wearing the ghastly apron I sewed for her in home ec, turquoise it was, with white rickrack. Chlorine? The President's Day weekend we stayed at the old Traymore Hotel in Atlantic City decades after the city's heyday but years before its rebirth as Las Vegas East. I was 12 and fell madly in love with the pool boy, Wayne. Pine needles? The secret trail behind one of the cabins at Camp Tamarac, the trail that led to

The Rock, where I learned how to smoke cigarettes.

I think books are hardwired like this for some of us. There's a high-speed connection between book and experience, between what we've read and how we've lived.

We only have to glance at a book, the way others catch a scent in the air, and we experience that moment in time when the book intersected with our lives. I see Richard Brautigan's *The Pill Versus The Springhill Mine Disaster* on my bookshelf. I haven't read it in thirty years, and I have the sneaking suspicion that if I tried to read it now I'd find it lacking in just about everything I've subsequently come to appreciate in poetry. But it's not just a book. It's a time in my life. I am standing on the shoulder of I-80 in Nebraska hitching my way across the country, going west on my own for the first time. I have only two books in my backpack, Brautigan and the *I Ching*. Annie Dillard's *The Living*? An impossibly rainy summer vacation in Bandon, Oregon, during which my then four-year-old son gets clobbered in the head with a boat oar, and we have to rush him to the 15-bed local hospital to get stitched up. James Clavell's *Shogun*? That solitary winter vacation I spend in my first house, the one with no central heating, curled up in an armchair by the window existing on pots of Seattle spice tea and packages of Archway chocolate chip cookies.

We have all read books that shifted reality for us, made us think of the world in a different way (Lewis Thomas' *Lives of a Cell*), or books that resonated deeply as they charted unfamiliar emotional terrain (May Sarton's *Journal of a Solitude*). We've read books that made our lives bigger, that transported us across time and space, across culture and gender, books that created entire worlds for us to explore and inhabit. Books have enormous, almost incalculable, intellectual and emotional power in our lives.

But there is more. There is this other kind of power: the power to mark our passages, to define us, to remind us who we were, what we cared about, what we dreamed, to evoke time and place and state of mind. My books, spine out on the shelves in my library, are entries in a diary I didn't know I was keeping.

In between the pages, too, are hints of life lived. I go to the shelf and pull out *My Mother, Myself*, the hardback edition published in 1977, which was a particularly nasty year in the already rocky relationship I had with my mother. Tucked in between pages 44 and 45 I find her photograph, one I must have stolen from an old album. My mother looks sweetly at the camera. She has a mop of dark, curly hair and is holding a doll. She is perhaps ten. In *Wild Alaska*, a Time-Life book with page after page of stunning Arctic pictures, I find a menu for a little restaurant I used to frequent a block from the Fullerton El, just around the corner from my fourth-floor walk-up. I read that book on the fire escape and dreamed of the great north during my last and sweatiest summer in Chicago. In Peter Matthiessen's *The Snow Leopard*, I find a postcard of a cheap motel in Battle Mountain, Nevada, where my car broke down – and where I stayed for five very long days while a part was sent from who-knows-where.

Now I see something peeking out of the pages of the French's mustard yellow beat-up paperback edition of *Zen Flesh, Zen Bones*, and, with great excitement, I pull the book from the shelf. What could it be? What could I have placed between the pages of this wonderful book, this book that made me think thoughts I had never thought before, this book that prompted me to sign up for my first yoga class, this book that I carried around like a talisman for years? I am ready to be wowed.

It's an appointment card. On Thursday, Sept. 24, 1997, I went to get my teeth cleaned.

2

IN PRAISE OF LIBRARIES

So many books, so little time

Everyone who loves libraries has a library story. Here's mine:

It begins in Brooklyn, New York, where I had the great fortune to live near my maternal grandparents for the first eight years of my life. My grandfather was a high school teacher and a talented watercolorist. My grandmother, who had not finished high school, was a voracious reader with an intense curiosity about the world. Their idea of fun, of a great vacation, was traveling across the country in their hulking 1948 Nash stopping at college campuses and signing up for summer courses.

This was decades before Elderhostel, two generations before the concept of the "nontraditional learner." There was no program for them. But there they were, a smiling middle-aged couple dressed in summer cottons, identical straw hats perched on their heads, asking to sit in on Modern European Poetry or The Civilization of Mesopotamia or Renaissance Architecture. My grandfather, the teacher, was the shy one. It was my grandmother who knocked on doors, made appointments with registrars, and cornered professors in the hallway. She was charming, cheerful, enthusiastic – and insistent. She never took no for an answer. Every summer, she managed to talk her way (and his) into a classroom somewhere.

Back home in New York in the late summer, they would resume their normal lives and take up once again their grandparently duties, which meant almost weekly visits with their only grandchild, me. Saturday mornings my mother would drop me off at my grandparents' apartment, and Saturday afternoon my grandmother and I would walk several blocks to the Brooklyn Public Library. It was a huge, dark building, scary and thrilling, busy yet noiseless. I loved it. My grandmother would use her library card to sign out a small stack of books for me.

When I was four, I asked for a library card of my own. The librarian took one look at me and shook her head. Sorry, she said, a cardholder has to be able to write his or her name – in *cursive* – to get a card. She leaned forward from her perch behind the counter when she said "in cursive." I had just recently learned to *print* my first name in large wobbly capital letters. But I wanted a card of my own, and my grandmother wanted me to have a card of my own, and my grandmother never took no for an answer. So together we practiced.

It took weeks of work, most of one of my grandfather's sketchpads and dozens of Crayolas. I would clench the crayon so tightly that it snapped halfway through the "L." My grandmother put her large, freckled hand over mine to guide me through the loops and swirls, and slowly my fingers relaxed and learned the motions. Then, one Saturday, I signed my name in cursive at the big mahogany library desk, and the librarian handed me my card. She said I was their youngest patron ever.

Since then, libraries have been a force in my life – as a reader, a student, a teacher and a writer, from the Lincoln room in the

Chicago Public Library to the basement of the old San Francisco library to the lovely old Carnegie library in McMinnville, Oregon, to the glorious new library built by the smart and generous citizens of the town I am lucky enough to inhabit.

As I nonfiction writer, I use libraries *hard*. For my last book, I had to teach myself, among other things, the history of the American Communist movement, the geography of Manhattan Island and the culture of Italy under Mussolini. For the book before that, I was in the library gathering armfuls of books on the history of aviation and the history of Hollywood. Before that, I gave myself, via the library, a crash course on the women's sports. And before that, tutorials on Meiji-era Japan, U.S. immigration policy and the apple industry. I have spent many, many hours in the library and many, many months at my desk reading the books I brought home.

I am not, I should note, a neoLuddite who spurns the internet. I cruise, peruse and use internet sources all the time. But for the real deal, the fully vetted information, the experts I can trust, for richness and depth, for portable wisdom I can read in bed at night or take with me on a trip, I go to books. I go to the library.

But I also appreciate libraries in a less pragmatic way. As a writer, I appreciate a library the way a painter appreciates a museum – a place of inspiration, a living monument to what I do. It is both exhilarating and humbling to be in the presence of thousands of books, surrounded not just by information but by knowledge, by art and culture, by stories.

A few years ago, I brought my then five-year-old daughter to a large, sprawling public library. She looked around, wide-eyed. Up to the ceiling and down to the floor, all she could see were books. She was momentarily – and uncharacteristically – speechless.

"Mommy," she said, after a while. "Did you write all these books?" (Isn't it wonderful what small children think we are capable of?)

"No," I said, kneeling down to give her a hug. She squirmed away to look up again at the ceiling-high shelves.

"Well," she said. "Did you *read* all these books?"

"I'm working on it," I told her.

3

CH-CH-CHANGES

The new (media) world order

I grew up in a household where two newspapers landed on the doorstep every morning. The mailman delivered *Newsweek* and *U.S. News & World Report* every week, and a half dozen other magazines made their way onto the living room coffee table every month. I learned about the world from Walter Cronkite and based my fifth grade term report ("Kansas: The Wheat State"...A+) on the entry in the *World Book Encyclopedia*. Downstairs in the den, the 20 white leatherette volumes competed for shelf space with my mother's ever-expanding collection of Book of the Month Club novels. I learned to love rock 'n' roll listening to the WMCA Good Guys on the little transistor radio I hid under my pillow every night. I learned to love movies watching old ones on Channel 9's *Million Dollar Movie*. I memorized scenes (Paul Henreid lighting a cigarette and passing it to Bette Davis) and dialog ("I don't think I will kiss you, although you need kissing, badly," Rhett says to Scarlett) because WOR ran the same movie twice every evening from Monday to Friday, and then three times a day on Saturday and Sunday.

I lived in a media-rich environment, 20th century-style. As a teen, I was under the powerful influence of the comic strip *Brenda Starr, Reporter* (flaming red hair, exotic boyfriend with patch over eye, intoxicating international adventures) and the Susan St. James character in the TV series *The Name of the Game* (perky, witty, winsome, works for handsome powerful boss at great magazine). Journalism sounded great. I went to journalism school. When I started as a freelancer, I got paid – not much, but something – for every word I wrote. When I started writing books, the expectation was bigger advances for every new project, book tours with escorts (no, not that kind), and an editor who was a book junkie, who loved words more than end-caps at B&N.

Those days are gone. Those days are so gone that they border on quaint. Those days are so gone that they qualify as "back in the day." Am I sad? Am I happy? Yes. Am I worried? Am I excited? Yes. Like many who are living through the recontouring of the media landscape, I have been rocked not just by the changes themselves but by my accompanying emotions.

I was thinking about all this a few days ago on a plane heading back to Oregon. My seatmate was listening to a book on her iPod while simultaneously window-shopping on eBay on her wifi-enabled tablet. I was listening to music on my iPhone (through noise-canceling headphones, of course) while working on an essay on my laptop. I thought about the media-rich virtual bubbles we can now easily create around ourselves and the road we have, both individually and collectively, traveled to get where we are. This has been, and continues to be, a cultural, economic – and *emotional* – journey we are on, a journey that began with the shock that our old media environment was ailing and in decline and is now progressing toward acceptance of an entirely new way of being. It is, I suddenly thought sitting on that plane, a journey not unlike the one mapped by psychiatrist Elisabeth Kübler-Ross.

In identifying what she called the Five Stages of Grief — Denial, Anger, Bargaining, Depression and Acceptance — Kübler-Ross attempted to deconstruct and understand how people dealt with significant and traumatic loss like the news that you have a terminal illness or the death of a loved one. But suppose it isn't your beloved aunt who has died...it is your beloved legacy media?

Which brings me to my New! Improved! *Seven* Stages of Grief over the death of the media world I knew as a child.

1. Denial: No! The world is not changing, dammit. As long as I sit here with my cup of coffee and my *New York Times*, everything is just the same as it ever was.

2. Confusion: Wait a minute: Something appears to be going on. Is the world changing? How? Why? What does this mean?

3. Anger: The world is changing, and someone is to blame! A new generation of illiterates! The school system! Corporate greed! Big Pharma! (Sorry, I just like to blame Big Pharma for everything.)

4. Disquietude: I don't understand this new world. Do I need to buy a whole bunch of new stuff to live in it? What stuff?

5. Nostalgia: Ah, the good old days of phones that were attached to the wall and the simple joys of being out of touch. Vinyl. Sigh.

6. Acceptance: I love Google Scholar (and Maps and Images) so much, I want to marry them. All of them. I am streaming *Big Love* through Netflix, so I know that's okay.

7. Exuberance: Yes! A new app for my tablet! Sweet.

4

THE FEW, THE PROUD, THE READERS

Are books absolutely necessary?

Here is a statistic that will make you gasp, or wince, or just break down and cry: One-third of Americans with college or graduate school degrees did not read a single (non work-related) book last year. *Not one book.* That's a 60 percent increase in educated non-readers in the past twenty years.

It's no surprise what these non-readers are doing. They are playing online and video games, watching YouTube, blogging, Instagramming, channel surfing. I get it. I mean, I don't get why hours of *Mortal Kombat, Assassin's Creed* or *Grand Theft Auto* could possibly be more compelling than reading just about any single sentence that Joan Didion has ever written, but I get that people are otherwise occupied.

But here's the disconnect – or the series of disconnects: As the percentage of people who read books has declined (precipitously) in all categories (young, old and in between, white, Black and Hispanic, men and women, educated and not), the number of book titles published in the U.S. has soared. A new book appears on

Amazon *every five minutes*. While readers have declined, the online retail space for books has exploded.

So, let me get this straight: More books. Quicker, more convenient access to book-buying than ever. Fewer readers. Oh, and one more fact to chew on: The number of self-declared "creative writers" has skyrocketed. More writers. Fewer readers. It is little wonder that eight out of every ten books published in the U.S. lose money. The leaky vessel that is the commercial publishing industry stays afloat courtesy of Stephen King, Danielle Steele, *Joy of Cooking*, the *King James Bible* – and the occasional Cheryl Strayed.

I am left dazed and confused, asking myself (and everyone around me who is not busy playing *WoW*) if this is the end of Western Civilization. (Not to mention the end of my career.) Suppose the numbers keep going the way they're going. Suppose in ten years, half of educated people don't read; in twenty years, two-thirds, and so on, until reading a book becomes as uncommon as, say, sitting through *Der Ring des Nibelungen*, or flossing twice a day. If hardly anyone reads, would that be so terrible?

I want to convince myself that we are not, as my grandma used to say, going to hell in a handbasket. And so, I reason that, on one level, reading a book is just a pastime, a hobby, a pleasant way to spend a rainy afternoon. Suppose that afternoon was spent not with book in hand but rather with mouse or remote in hand. Big deal. It's hard to get all apocalyptic about that. On another level, reading a book is a pretty decent way to learn about people, places, events, issues, and low-fat cuisine. But with Google searching 350 zillion sites in less time than it takes to turn the page of a book, with Wikipedia on top of the culture as it evolves, with blogs commenting daily, even hourly, who needs to wait two years for a book to make it from inside the author's head to the new releases table?

Ah, but reading a book is not just a way to while away a few hours and not just a method of gleaning information, it is an act of engagement. Books, good ones, can simultaneously tweak emotion and intellect. They can make us feel and think, dream and imagine. A book can transport a reader back and forward in time, across continents and oceans (and galaxies), and deep inside psyches. If we continue down the path of becoming a nation of nonreaders, do we miss out on these extraordinary experiences? I would like to say *yes!* because I am a life-long, utterly committed bibliophile who cannot imagine a life without books. But the fact is, nonreaders who encounter other art forms – a piece of music, for example, or a painting – might experience this same sense of engagement, this same swelling of the spirit and quickening of mind.

So here I am, making the case that books are not absolutely necessary, that the frightening statistics about our growing national aversion to reading are not all that frightening, that civilization will not, in fact, come tumbling down around our ears if very few of us read books. And yet, I remain unconvinced by my own arguments – and I hope you do too

…because there is something else going on with books, with, not to be too precious about it, The Book. The Book is a unique cultural artifact. It is creativity and imagination, analysis and synthesis, wit, insight, sensitivity, perception, ingenuity and epiphany – and you get to hold it in your hands. You get to own it. You get to sink into it any time you want. Wow. Obviously I am not talking about *Thin Thighs in Thirty Days* or *Chicken Soup for the Cat Lover's Soul.* But neither am I limiting my admiration to Shakespeare or Pliny the Elder (I hear the Younger was no slouch either). Inspiration- and epiphany-wise, these guys are great. But I am a reader and writer of modern narrative nonfiction. My touchstones are books like *A River Runs Through It* and *The Year of*

Magical Thinking. These are the nuanced, textured, deeply experienced, wisely told tales to which I resonate. And it is precisely these characteristics – nuance, texture, wisdom – that I believe make books necessary, essential, and irreplaceable.

I don't know how to reverse the statistics, how to make book-lovers out of the one-third of us who don't read. But I do think that the two-thirds of us who still do read ought to stay the course despite the cultural storms and the CyberSirens singing to us from the rocks. It's up to us two-thirds to read more, to join or form book clubs, to support our libraries, to keep independent booksellers alive – and to good keep writers gainfully employed.

5

FACT, FABLE, AND MEMOIR

Can writers have it both ways?

James Frey's editor said she didn't know. James Frey's literary agent said she didn't know. James Frey's publisher said she didn't know. James Frey's readers said, apparently, they didn't care. Or didn't care enough to stop buying his memoir-in-dispute, *A Million Little Pieces*, which held its place on the *New York Times* bestseller list during a several week-long literary storm that should have capsized the book. Oprah said she didn't care; then she changed her mind and said she did care. A lot.

Like Oprah, the *New York Times* appeared to care a little too much – front page stories, columns, op-eds, day after day – covering the unfolding story with that barely disguised glee the media save for reporting on the missteps and misdeeds of media other than themselves. National TV, national radio, websites, blogs and just about every newspaper in the country focused on exactly what James Frey pretended to have experienced for the sake of dramatic storytelling (three months in jail, root canals without anesthesia) versus what he actually did experience (three nights in jail, standard dental treatment).

Questions were asked: What percentage of *A Million Little Pieces* was imagined rather than lived? Is it acceptable to play fast and loose with facts if the underlying message, the core truth, is untarnished? Was Frey's literary agent complicit in what everyone seemed to agree was a deception (including, on Oprah, Mr. Frey himself) because she submitted the manuscript first as fiction and then as nonfiction? And how could an old pro like publisher Nan Talese appear to care so little about the veracity of the work she published as nonfiction? And, while we're at it, why didn't Random House engage in even the most basic fact-checking on a book whose power derived from its factuality?

All good questions. But not the question that was stumping me as I followed this story. That question was: *Why was everyone so surprised to learn that a memoir was more fable than fact?*

I consider it self-evident that memoir is not nonfiction. How can it be? Memoirs are crafted of selective memory, the product of insight-after-the-fact, of impressions made long ago. They are the stories people tell about themselves, and, whether they know it or not, whether they mean to or not, they tell these stories how they wish the stories were, how they need them to be, how they choose to interpret and understand the events of their lives. Memoirs, especially "trauma memoirs" like Frey's, are often undertaken as therapy. The author – frequently not a professional writer – has lived through something big and bad, how big and how bad being a matter of self-perception (or deception), of how much the memoirist cares to know or find out about him or herself, of how much the experience has been understood, of how much responsibility the memoirist takes for the life he or she has lived.

Memoirs are not about research, fieldwork, and fact-finding, the methods nonfiction authors employ to gather the material they will write about. When Frank McCourt, to take one celebrated trauma memoirist, writes a detailed anecdote about bicycling through the street of Limerick to deliver a telegram some sixty-plus years ago, he bases his narrative not on interviews with the people involved in the story, not on archival research, not on letters or diaries or photographs or any kind of document. He writes what he remembers. Or thinks he remembers. Or what could have happened that he doesn't quite remember. Or what makes a good story.

Filling in the blanks of an experience – writing that your sister's dress was red when, for the life of you, you can't remember what color it was, or that the house was cold and damp on that long ago day when you don't remember but you assume it must have been because the house was often cold and damp – is taking liberties where liberties should probably not be taken. But what James Frey did was different. James Frey fabricated entire experiences. He contrived events. He wrote, in detail, about things that never happened. He intentionally rewrote his personal history to appear tougher and badder than he was, more worthy of pity or respect or whatever emotion he needed to pull from readers to make himself whole again.

With Frey's book, it's an easy call. *A Million Little Pieces* is a fictionalized version of the author's experiences, what is called a *roman à clef* – a novel. That the manuscript was rejected as a novel because the writing wasn't good enough and the story arc was overly melodramatic says something about the quality readers will accept in what is labeled a memoir.

This year Frey was the poster child for fabrication . Ten years ago it was Lorenzo Carcaterra and his *Sleepers: A True Story* (not) about growing up in Hell's Kitchen. In between, there was Jennifer Lauck's *Blackbird*, a grim childhood memoir that her half-brother contended was half-truth, and Dave Pelzer's *A Child Called*

It, the revolting and sordid details of which have recently come under question.

It's wasted effort to rake these memoirists over the coals for the sins of prevarication, fabrication, and exaggeration. Let's just stipulate that memoir, by its very nature (highly subjective personal stories) and by its methods (remembering rather than researching) is not nonfiction. The goal of memoir is not to carefully and conscientiously piece together a factual tale but rather (as Oprah tried to argue and then backed away from) to explore an underlying truth.

If a writer wants the freedom to change the details, to describe events that never happened, create characters who never lived, imagine and invent rather than research and uncover, the writer has made a choice. The choice is called fiction. Come clean with us readers. We can take it. As a reader (and as a writer), I do not think writers have to sacrifice facts for good, powerful storytelling. I think the two are entirely compatible. This is what good literary nonfiction is. Memoir is not bad nonfiction, or faulty nonfiction. It is simply not nonfiction at all.

6

NONFICTION NEVER-NEVER LAND

Fantasy trumps reality

It's bad enough that it's called nonfiction, named for what it isn't rather than what it is, as if we decided to call poetry *nonprose*, or day *nonnight*.

It's bad enough that some practitioners of this genre that has no proper name of its own have undermined its credibility, chipping away at its special power of authenticity by fabrication and invention, or dulling its fine edge by substituting memory for research and reporting. Now there's something else to be concerned about: It may be that fans of this beleaguered genre don't actually want nonfiction at all. They want fantasy.

Here's my recent ah-ha moment on that subject: I had just bought and started reading a wonderful book called *Tales of a Female Nomad*. It's the story of a woman who took to traveling the world by herself after her marriage fell apart. The book came out in 2001 and made barely a ripple in the publishing pond.

This is a thoughtful book about an ordinary woman who didn't just face and come to terms with her loneliness and vulnerability – that's embedded in the book but is not the point. It is a book about embracing and learning from cultures, about trusting strangers, about learning to be at home in the world. As I read this largely forgotten book, I couldn't stop thinking about another seemingly similar woman's travel narrative, a publishing sensation, *Eat, Pray, Love*, which maintained a #1 spot on the *New York Times* paperback nonfiction best-seller list for a long time. It was a BookSense bestseller, an Oprah rave, and a book group fave.

Both of these books are adventure travel memoirs written by smart women who want to learn something from their experiences. Yet the gulf between them is unswimmable: One is nonfiction; the other is fantasy.

In *Nomad,* a middle-aged woman – from her author photo, she looks to be both plain and plump – weathers the end of an almost three-decades-long marriage, says goodbye to her two grown (and very worried) children, puts herself on a $15,000 a year budget, and travels the globe for more than a decade, funding her peripatetic life by writing the occasional children's book.

In *Eat, Pray, Love,* a very pretty thirty-something woman with a thriving writing career recovers from the kind of bad marriage one can have in one's twenties (no kids, baggage light enough to be of the carry-on variety) by indulging her senses with stays in Italy, India, and Indonesia. The author of *Eat, Pray, Love* sets out on her several-month adventure funded by a six-figure book advance.

The gulf between the two books only widens from there.

In the first scene of *Female Nomad,* our heroine is sitting in her economy hotel room in Cuernavaca, exhausted and hungry. She wants dinner, but she is too intimidated to go to a restaurant by herself. She imagines sitting alone at a table. People will look at her. She'll feel awkward and uncomfortable. She calls down for room service and learns there is none. So she takes a cab to a better-class hotel and hangs out in the lobby waiting to see if she can make a connection with a friendly person whom she can enlist as a dinner mate.

Eat, Pray, Love, on the other hand, opens with our self-assured heroine wondering if she should have an affair with the gorgeous young guy she meets at cafes several times a week to practice her Italian. No, perhaps it's too early to consider this, she reasons. Instead she flirts and eats, flirts and eats. And eats. She is happy – happy! – to gain twenty-four pounds during the Italian part of her adventure because, well, she *needed* to gain the weight. Can you guess yet which book I classify as nonfiction and which as fantasy?

In the appealing (and beautifully written) *Eat, Pray, Love*, the author gets in touch with her hedonistic self in Italy, achieves enlightenment in India (a land-speed record, I might add) and, in Indonesia, hooks up with a dashing, wealthy older man who wants nothing more than the privilege of adoring her.

Meanwhile, our *Nomad* is being questioned by nasty guards at the El Salvador border, examining her ambivalence toward her own Jewishness in Israel, learning about the caste system in Bali and, country by country, year by year, opening her heart and mind to the cultures of the world. She doesn't reach satori or find the love of her life. Instead, she slowly, slowly, becomes a better person.

Readers ran, cash in hand, to buy hundreds of thousands of copies of the fantasy book (that would be the one in which the woman gains weight and is happy about it). They pretty much ignored the nonfiction book. The legions of *E, P, L* readers wanted a "true" story – after all, they bought nonfiction not a novel – but really they wanted a dream. They wanted to read about the luminous young woman who found everything she was looking for – everything *any* woman could possibly be looking for – in six months flat. They were uninterested in reading about the earnest middle-aged woman who camped out in youth hostels and lived out of her backpack while venturing deeply into other people's lives.

This bothers me – the enormous popularity of the fantasy, the blip on the screen of the other book – not because I do not like fantasy. I do. And not because I did not like *E, P, L*. I did. It bothers me because nonfiction has a hard enough time making its way in the world without that kind of competition. Books like *E, P, L* raise the bar for readers' expectations. They will not be satisfied with stories of mere mortals making their hesitant way through the world. They want writers who look like movie stars living out the kind of adventures that virtually no one but that well-funded writer has or ever will have.

This reminds me of Norm the carpenter. He was on a program I used to watch religiously called *This Old House*. The home improvement show was, I think, the first of its kind and was, for a while, wildly popular with the PBS crowd. Norm the carpenter was an ordinary-looking guy – okay, less than ordinary – maybe in his late forties. He was bulky without being buff, wore dorky glasses and dorkier shirts and spoke with an annoyingly nasal Boston accent. He was a great carpenter, though, a hard worker. He really listened to the home owners whose houses he was helping to remodel. For most of the show, you could see him hefting boards or mortising joints or setting windows. Here was a guy you could trust, the kind of workman you wouldn't hesitate to leave alone in your house.

But who would want Norm the carpenter now when they could have the deliciously swarthy hottie who stars on *Take Home Handyman* or the *GQ*-like hunk on *Trading Spaces*, his tool belt slung low over slender hips, his hair expertly rumpled, as if he just got out of bed (yours?). Fantasy carpenters! Can they use a miter saw? Drive a straight nail? Who cares!

Our heads are full of fantasy that masquerades as reality: the sexy carpenter, the beautiful author to whom all good and amazing things happen. And then, of course, the endless sea of heavily plotted, heavily edited "reality" shows. Reality, which (I admit) sometimes is not so great anyway, is now seeming even dingier, drabber, less exciting, less worthy of our attention. When fantasy is consistently, doggedly presented as reality, poor, embattled nonfiction has to face yet another opponent, one that it is mighty hard to defeat.

7

A MAN IN FULL

Giving Tom Wolfe his due

I write in praise of Tom Wolfe.

He is, I know, a hard guy to like – a smug, snooty patrician in a silly white suit with a look on his face that says *I'm better than you are, and we both know it.* I mean, what kind of an intellectual braggart can claim in a single working lifetime to have both created a new literary genre and resuscitated an old one?

Forty years ago Wolfe (rightly) accused American journalism of being unequal to the task of chronicling the weird place America had become. He and several of his New York cronies were experimenting with a brand of scene-setting, storytelling journalism that better suited the times, he said. Never mind that others, many others, had been practicing the form long before he came on the scene (anyone for John Hersey? Truman Capote? Charles Dickens? Daniel freaking Defoe?), Wolfe claimed ownership and exercised the father's prerogative: He named the form – New Journalism – and proceeded to practice it, in newspapers, magazines and series of oddly titled books, through the late 1960s into the late 70s.

Okay, so he didn't *invent* New Journalism. And claiming that he did showed both an overblown ego and an underdeveloped sense of history (and this from a guy with a Ph.D. in American Studies from Yale). But there's no denying that Wolfe was one of New Journalism's consummate practitioners. From his hyperkinetic re-creation of Ken Kesey and the Merry Pranksters' cross-country bus trip (*Electric Kool-Aid Acid Test*), which captured '60s counterculture like no other piece of writing ever has, to his astute exploration of the inner world of early astronauts (*The Right Stuff*), Wolfe has shown himself a master of subculture reporting. His eye is keen; his wit is sharp, his approach fresh, vibrant, and outrageous. Almost always, his intelligence trumps his arrogance.

Kurt Vonnegut called him a genius. Terry Southern proclaimed him, in the argot of times past, a "groove and a gas." He is "more than brilliant…more than urbane, suave, trenchant…Tom Wolfe is a goddamn joy," gushed one critic. To that I say: *Yes, yes, yes.* And so I am inclined to forgive him both his lapse of memory about the origins of the genre he claims as his own and his, as Anatole Broyard so cuttingly put it, "cheap capital letters, adjectives yoked together by violence and spastic punctuation." Pish, posh. The man is dazzling.

At the top of his game twenty years ago, Wolfe changed direction, first publishing an inflammatory essay proclaiming that the Great American Novel was not all that great anymore – and then setting out to personally rectify the sad state of American letters. What made him dazzling as a reporter now made him equally dazzling as a novelist. *Bonfire of the Vanities* may have erred on the side of parody (and been damaged by a horrendous film adaptation), but *A Man in Full* was pitch-perfect and *I am Charlotte Simmons* is both as flawed as critics say and sinfully, outrageously good.

So he hasn't, as promised, single-handedly resurrected the Balzacian novel. But he writes some of the smartest social commentary around. And he has done something that few others have: He has successfully, masterfully translated his skills as a reporter into a career as a major novelist. In fact, it's clear that he remains indebted to his reportorial past. For *I am Charlotte Simmons*, for example, Wolfe did all the legwork he would have done had he been working on a piece of New Journalism. He spent significant time at a number of college campuses around the country, observing, listening, interviewing, part sociologist, part cultural anthropologist, part journalist, immersing himself in the strange and disturbing subculture that is American college life in the 21st century.

His unsparing, ruthlessly amusing and, for those of us in the know, *dead-on*, portrayal of everyone from college athletes to college intellectuals to PC professors is the work of a man in full. His biting send-up of *U.S. News and World Report's* college ratings is a gem. And his hilarious linguistic exploration of the many and astonishingly varied uses of the words *shit* and *fuck* in the college students' vocabulary (Wolfe calls this speaking the "shit patois" or the "fuck patois") is the product of a writer deeply, seamlessly, gloriously embedded in the world he is chronicling.

Wolfe's years as a reporter taught him how to listen, which may be the single most important talent – yes, it is a *talent* – a writer can cultivate. And so as a novelist, he listens not only to what all novelists claim to listen to (The Muse) but to real live people. He is out in the world seeking material to create a literary world that is both just shy of being factual and undeniably true. As a New Journalist, he helped pioneer (and, as is his wont, name) the use of what he called "status detail," the sharply observed everyday habits of people, to explore character. Again, this talent transfers beautifully to fiction.

Reading Tom Wolfe the journalist and Tom Wolfe the novelist shows just how close literary nonfiction is to literature. And how, in the right hands, both can lay equal claim to being important, resonant chroniclers of the human condition.

It also helps answer the question posed earlier: *What kind of an intellectual braggart can claim in a single working lifetime to have both created a new literary genre and resuscitated an old one?* Answer (with minor reservations and quibbles): One who has.

8

THE TALENTED MR. TALESE

All hail the master

What can you say about a guy who writes a sentence like this:

It was not quite spring, the silent season before the search for salmon, and the old fishermen of San Francisco were either painting their boats or repairing their nets along the pier or sitting in the sun talking quietly among themselves, watching the tourists come and go, and smiling now, as a pretty girl paused to take their picture.

The soft sibilance of the five "s" sounds that whoosh and whisper – and then quit just before it gets to be too much. The lilting sentence, with its graceful parade of clauses that mimic the rhythm of a camera panning a scene. The scene itself: simple, direct, with exactly, precisely, the right detail. The way the camera, and the sentence, both stop as the pretty girl stops, and the action pauses.

What can you say about a guy who writes a sentence like this:

The tallest man in New York, Edward Carmel, stands 8 feet 2 inches, weighs 475 pounds, eats like a horse and lives in the Bronx.

The glorious matter-of-factness of that. The astonishing

statistics presented in monotone, the silly cliché, the surprise ba-boom of "the Bronx." It's a pitch-perfect introduction that meshes extraordinary with ordinary.

Or what about a guy who distills the essence of a time, a place and a subculture with this eat-your-heart-out-*Devil-Wears-Prada* sentence:

Each weekday morning a group of suave and wrinkle-proof women, who call each other "dear" and "dahling" and can speak in italics and curse in French, move into Manhattan's Graybar Building, elevate to the nineteenth floor, and then slip behind their desks at Vogue...

Come on. Wrinkle-proof? (He could have written "unwrinkled.") Speaking in italics? (He could have written "speaking emphatically.") "Elevating" to the nineteenth floor? (He could have written "take the elevator.") But he didn't. And you know why? Because he is a master.

This is a guy who can make the life of a shy, balding obit writer as compellingly readable, as deeply engrossing as the life of Frank Sinatra, a man who makes equal sense of bridge builders and Broadway directors, newspaper executives and massage parlor owners, Italian immigrants and Black prize fighters.

This is Gay Talese. And what you can say about him is what Mario Puzo, of *Godfather* fame, once said about him: He is the best nonfiction writer in America.

In his generation of pioneering literary journalists, Tom Wolfe was flashier; Joan Didion was brainier; Jimmy Breslin was ballsier; and Truman Capote was...well, Truman Capote. But Talese, Talese was the best. Is the best. Classy. Original. Unpretentious. Sharp and observant without nastiness. Elegant without frills. Empathetic but no patsy. Smart but no show-off.

I bought my first Talese book, a paperback edition of *Fame and Obscurity*, at a used bookstore in San Francisco for $1.25. I had never heard of the guy. I had never heard of literary journalism.

After four years at Medill School of Journalism slogging my way through inverted pyramid news stories and another six months writing drek for a little newspaper, I had had it with journalism. It wasn't about writing. It was about ordering information. It wasn't about people. It was about sources. Why – I asked myself after I quit the paper and started selling crafts on Embarcadero Square – did I ever want to be a journalist in the first place?

Talese answered that question for me.

And still does.

9

R.I.P.

The Book, 1454-2008(?)

The book is dead.

That's the title of the book I'm currently reading. Of course the fact that this book was written and published, that I bought it and am reading it would seem a powerful argument against its main premise.

In fact, 172,000 books were published in the U.S. in 2008, the year after *The Book is Dead* was published. (Most recent figures? More than 300,000 new books a year.) If you count self-published books and print-on-demand, a new book of fiction is right now being published every 30 seconds in America. How can the book be dead?

There are several good answers to this. First of all, most of those hundred thousand-plus books (or, today, three times as many) are essentially moribund, gathering dust in the acres of unexplored digital space on Amazon. When *The Book is Dead* was first published eight long years ago, and Amazon was less of the behemoth bookseller it is today, more people left their houses and went to actual bookstores. But as a B&N honcho said back then, the miles of aisles stocked with books were merely "wallpaper" – background decoration so that the place felt literary. The people coming in to buy one of perhaps 20 "it" books wanted to browse for a while, sit in an armchair, sip a latte, and feel ensconced in the world of books – of which eight out of ten flop in the marketplace. They die – mostly swiftly – moved from the front of the store "new" table to back shelf in three weeks, from shelf to return carton in two months and from there to $1.95 online sellers and Costco remainder bins.

But Sherman Young, the Australian academic who wrote *The Book is Dead*, is mourning the book for other reasons. He argues that the seemingly crowded literary marketplace is mostly jammed with what he calls "functional books" and "anti-books" – not *real* books. Real books are well and lovingly crafted, emotionally and intellectually resonant. They are the work of people who think and care – authors, editors and publishers – people passionate about both words and ideas. This sort of literary endeavor is dying the author argues.

Functional books, on the other hand, are flourishing. These are the instructional and inspirational tomes that frequently top the best-seller list. You know the titles, from the recent *You: On a Diet* to the venerable *What Color is My Parachute?* There's *Who Moved My Cheese* and *The Seven Habits of Highly Effective People* and Just-about-Anything *for Dummies*. There are mega-selling cookbooks (*Better Homes and Garden Cookbook*: 38 million) and franchises like *Chicken Soup for the* fill-in-the-blank *Soul*.

What the author calls "anti-books" are also on the rise. These are products manufactured for the marketplace – "cynical creations," the author says, and I agree – whose existence owes more to sales potential, synergy, cross-marketing and platform exploitation than to the quality (or for that matter, the existence) of the ideas within. Think O.J. Simpson's blessedly recalled (but unfortunately republished) *If I Did It.* Celebrity memoir and autobiography fit nicely here. In fact, most books on any subject written by – or about – a celebrity fit here, the idea being that consumers will buy the name whatever the product might be. (A Michael Jordan lunchbox, a Michael Jordan autobiography…it's all the same.) The name itself sells the product – or the celebrity, him- or herself directly sells the product (as in, for example, the egregious advice books written and then shilled on the radio by anti-feminist zealot and call-in show host Dr. Laura Schlessinger).

There are also a growing number of books that owe their existence to an aggressively entrepreneurial strain of literary agent known as the Book Packager. This is a person who, rather than waiting for worthwhile, publishable proposals to come his or her way like the other hard-working, God-fearing literary agents do, instead becomes a book "producer" by glomming onto hot topics, snagging an expert to attach his or her name to the project, corralling an out-of-work writer to write the text and selling the "package" to a publisher. Recent packaged projects include *The Elvis Treasures* (Yes! There are many.) and *Doga.* (I regret to inform you that this is a book about yoga for dogs.)

Functional books and anti-books do little to support what the author of *The Book is Dead* calls "Book Culture," the great and ongoing human conversation about what matters that takes place between the covers of books and among the people who read them. But nowadays these conversations are taking place in other media, often online, and the book has become (he argues) increasingly irrelevant to how we learn about the world and experience our culture. He is not arguing that the ideas in books are irrelevant, or the collected wisdom, or the resonant emotions. He is arguing that the book as *delivery system* that has seen its day.

I get it. Books are expensive and time-consuming to produce.

They are an environmental nightmare, made of paper, which comes from trees that are cut down, transported by gas-guzzling log trucks to stinky factories where energy-sucking machinery pulps them into the mush that becomes the pages that, after transport to another stinky factory, go through other energy-sucking machines that stain them with the combination of chemical dye and petroleum-based solvent known as ink. These objects are packed in thick paper boxes and loaded onto trucks that barrel down interstate highways taking the cargo to big warehouses, later to be transported to megastores or, via your internet-placed order, to be placed in the back of a truck that makes a private stop right in your own driveway.

It is difficult, even for a book-lover (not to mention book-writer) like myself to argue in favor of the book-as-delivery-system given all this.

But let me give it a shot.

From a reader's point of view, the book is a terrifically tidy little package, handy, portable and accessible in practically all conditions at all times. It is user-friendly (no instructions needed!) and ergonomic. It doesn't break down. It doesn't depend on electricity or batteries. Barring catastrophes (a house fire, your little brother overturning your inner tube in the pool while you're reading *Atlas Shrugged*), a book will last as long as you need or want it to. It can be collected or traded. It can be used as both gift and door stop. (But not at the same time, one hopes.)

From a researcher's point of view, there is no delivery system yet available that is as convenient. You can flip back and forth with abandon. You can dog-ear pages for future reference. Underline or highlight the good parts. Write notes in the margin. You can do this anywhere – in a tent by the river, on a lounge chair in your backyard – without electricity, without special equipment, hard- or software, or any device other than the lowly and dependable pencil.

But the key to my defense of the book is that the book is not just an idea-delivery system, it is a significant cultural artifact and a free-standing work of art. I am talking about the book itself, the object, apart from what exists as text. Book cover design is an art; interior page design is an art; typography is an art. I admit it. I am one of those typography-geeks who reads the colophon in the back of the book. (For the non-geeks among you, that's the final-page statement that tells you about what type was used and who invented it.) One of my books, for example, was set in Sabon (designed by a 20th century German typographer who named it for a famous 16th century typefounder); another was set in Ehrhardt (based on the design of a 17th century Hungarian type designer). This is great stuff! I feel richer for knowing this. I feel that my work is connected across centuries to these men.

So I have a modest proposal that will both help the environment and honor the world of the book-as-art:

Have publishers use alternative delivery systems for functional books. Functional books are not works of art. They do not endure. Users – which, for these books is a better descriptor than readers – can download the material to the device of their choice, thus saving paper, trees, oil, etc.

As for the anti-books: Don't publish them at all. Okay, so that's not exactly a modest proposal. But so many of these books are so entirely brainless, soulless, and artless, such bald-faced efforts at marketing and branding that I'm willing to tweak the First Amendment a bit and ban them. That would leave only the *real* books – perhaps 10,000 a year rather than 170,000 (or 300,000+). This would preserve and honor the world of the *real* book while yielding a much more delicate – and defensible – carbon footprint.

Am I right, or am I right?

10

READERS, READERS EVERYWHERE

Literature is alive in the provinces

With all the talk about how no one reads anymore and how the book is dead – I've gnashed teeth, wrung hands and written about this myself – I'd like to report back from the hinterlands that *it ain't so*. To paraphrase Mark Twain: The news of the death of literature has been greatly exaggerated. We writers may not have to abandon our craft and rush out to get honest employment – or take on PR clients.

What is the source of my wild optimism? It's called Oregon Reads, a statewide program that took place in nearly every public library and in every county in my home state of Oregon during our sesquicentennial celebration (that's 150 years). Masterminded by those mild-mannered defenders of the faith, those bi-focaled bastions of literacy, the state's librarians, the program was amazingly, exuberantly, vibrantly successful.

The librarians chose three Oregon-centric books – a work of narrative nonfiction, a young adult novel and a children's book –

wrote grants, beat the bushes and otherwise raised funds to buy thousands of copies of these books. Libraries, through the work of their dedicated foundations, also raised funds. (Let's pause a moment here to marvel at the fact that people are using their time and energy to fundraise for literature – and that these efforts have actually been successful, especially in these trying economic times.)

The result was the purchase and distribution of thousands and thousands of these books, boxes of books, pallets of boxes, sent to major metropolitan libraries and tiny old Carnegie libraries, libraries in wealthy suburbs and out in cowboy country, in coastal retirement communities and in dying timber towns. Many of these libraries not only acquired and distributed these books (for free) but hosted a variety of public programs in their communities. At these programs, which ran from January through April of the sesquicentennial year, sometimes as many as 600 people gathered in an auditorium to listen to an author talk about her book.

I know. I was privileged – honored – to be the author of one of the three books chosen for Oregon Reads. The book, a work of narrative nonfiction, was *Stubborn Twig*, a story of the promise and peril of becoming "American," an immigrant story, an Oregon pioneer story, told through the lives of three generations of a single family. I spoke in eighteen venues, from community rooms in libraries to school auditoriums to converted movie theatres, and everywhere I went there was excitement.

Excitement.

Not just about the book everyone was reading but about stories, about the power of stories in our lives, about how stories can tell us who we are and who we were. And equal excitement about libraries and their essential place in the life of communities. I was – I continue to be – flabbergasted by the intensity of involvement, by readers I thought did not exist, by librarians who have not slackened their pace despite budget cuts and understaffing, by businesspeople who donated money, who in some towns I visited hosted me in their hotels (a shout out here to the amazing Geiser Grand Hotel in Baker City, Oregon).

At each of the public events, I was deluged with questions. People wanted to know why I wrote what I wrote, where I got my ideas, how I did my research, how I wrote. They were hungry to understand the life of a writer and the life of a book. They followed me out of the library. They emailed me the next day. And no, it wasn't creepy. It was wonderful.

And so I am back from the hinterlands, from Pendleton and Ashland, Lincoln City, Hood River and Bend – from those small cities and smaller towns that no one outside of Oregon even knows the name of – and I am, like the new immigrants I wrote about in *Stubborn Twig,* "overblown with hope."

There are readers out there, plenty of them.

LAUREN KESSLER

THE ART OF WRITING

11

THE TEN STUPID THINGS WRITERS DO TO MESS UP THEIR LIVES

Ah, the fine art of self-sabotage

Consider me the Dr. Laura of writing. (I'm not talking politics here; I'm talking attitude.) Just like the shrill, conservative radio show call-in shrink you love to hate – author of such enlightened volumes as *The Ten Stupid Things Women Do to Mess Up Their Lives* (having a career being one of them) – I will show you no mercy. I will confront you with your own folly. I will force you to take the responsibility you are so quick to off-load on others: bad editors, unruly children, unsympathetic partners, the people in your writing group who *just don't understand what you're trying to do*

Discouraged? Dismayed? Disheartened? De- or re-jected? Get a grip. You'll get no sympathy from me. Writers are renowned for acts of self-sabotage, from extended experiments in procrastination to epic bouts of self-pity. You chose this ridiculous profession – or it chose you – so quit whining.

Face it: You need more than good ideas and literary talent. You need to learn to stop shooting yourself in the foot. Here are ten stupid things writers do to mess up their lives. Whichever apply to you – and I *know* several will – it's time to get smart about your writing life and stop undermining your best efforts.

#1
"I'll just 'clear the decks' before I start writing."

You know what? The decks will *never* be cleared. There will always be another call to make, another load of laundry to put in the washer, the emails in your in-box, those pesky weeds overrunning your garden. Life doesn't stop, or simplify itself, to allow you time to write. Life, in fact, has an uncanny way of getting in the way of writing. But that's only if you construct your days around everything you have to do that is *not* writing. If you construct your days around writing, then the question is not "when will I have time to sit down and write?" but rather "when will I have time to vacuum the living room carpet?" It's a sure bet that at the end of the day — and at the end of your life – you won't be wishing you spent more time with the Hoover. So learn to work with cluttered decks. And, most important, make writing the focus of your day, the core around which chores and errands fit – or don't.

#2
"It's time for me to have coffee with my writer friends."

Oh no, it isn't. It's time for you to apply the seat of the pants to the seat of the chair and get some work done. I don't mean writers should be without friends or, worse yet, without that tall nonfat extra hot latte. But it is all too easy to dissipate energy in conversation, spending irreplaceable writing time *talking* about writing rather than doing it. The hour-long phone chat comparing rejection letters, the long lunch gossiping about who got what published where, the potluck dinner where everyone talks about what they plan to write if they could only find the time – *give it up*. Don't talk away your enthusiasm or your ideas. Hoard your energy and use it to write.

#3

"A writing seminar on Crete?
The hills of Tuscany? Sign me up."

Sure, go ahead…if you want a vacation and freelancing has been so good to you (!) that you can afford it. But if you want to write, stay put. Exotic seminars are dilettantes' playgrounds not writers' workplaces.

#4

"I'll just keep writing until I run out of material."

It took me years to figure this one out: Don't bop 'til you drop. Although you may be physically capable of writing until you exhaust all your ideas, you sabotage your work in two ways by pushing too hard. First, the work you do at the ragged end of a writing jag is not going to be your best work. But even more important, writing until you run out of material means the next morning, when you get to your desk, you will be starting cold. And, as you stare at the screen or the pad of paper, you will be remembering that the reason you stopped writing was because you couldn't think of anything more to say. This is not an auspicious way to begin your day. Stop writing after you've put in a few good hours but *before* you stop thinking. Stop writing when you know what's coming next.

#5

"I'll just pass this new story by (choose one or more) my mother, my brother, my four closest friends, everyone in my writing group to see what they think."

Maybe you are lucky enough to have friends or writing compatriots whose opinions you trust. That's great. But remember, the more people you ask to comment and edit, the more comments and edits you get. One friend loves a scene; another thinks it doesn't work. Your mother wants you to flesh out the main character. Your brother wants you to kill her off on page 4. Three people in your writing group love your title; four hate it. Do you really need all this advice?

No. The opinion you need to trust is your own. I'm not saying that presenting your work to others is a bad idea. I'm saying other people's opinions should not substitute for your own. You can't depend on others to tell you what you've done, or not done. You can't depend on others to make you work harder or feel better about your work. You must learn to depend on yourself. The way to do that is to stop giving away the responsibility to others.

Of course, sometimes you have to *share* the responsibility. That's called working with an editor.

#6

"Revision? Whaddya mean? I got it right the first time."

On the other end of the spectrum from those who foist their manuscripts on friends, relatives, neighbors and people they meet in the cereal aisle are those writers who don't even pass their stories by their *own* eyes. Hey: It's written; it's spell-checked; it's out the door.

There are a number of equally inexcusable reasons for this bad behavior. Maybe you haven't given yourself the time to properly revise your work. Or maybe you don't yet understand how important revision is to good writing. Revision isn't an afterthought. It isn't a quick once-over. It is an essential process that gives you the opportunity not merely to correct errors but to re-think, re-structure and re-invent. Or maybe you think the piece is so good it doesn't need revision (Go immediately to Stupid Thing #9).

#7
"Please…I'm an artist, not a businessperson."

I know. It's unfair that we have to both create the stuff *and* sell it. And, gulp, ourselves. But that's the way this enterprise works. Knowing how to assess the market, how to write a savvy proposal or a targeted pitch, working social media, learning how to run your little operation like a CEO, understanding contracts, taking advantage of tax breaks – this is all a part of being a published writer, like it or not.

#8
"It won't matter that I'm a week late with the manuscript."

Oh yes it will. Maybe not now. Maybe not with this editor. But some day, and for the rest of your life.

#9
"This is the best thing I've ever written.
I am a true creative genius."

It may be the best thing you've ever written, or – watch out! –

the muse may have you by the throat. It is when we are most inspired that we are least objective about our work. Let this piece, which will surely bring you the Nobel Prize for Literature, sit a few days. Let your ardor cool and your hubris deflate. Give yourself time to forget just how long you labored over that turn-of-the-phrase. You know, the one that a few days from now will appear somewhat less clever than you originally thought. Or what about that dialog that just seemed to "write itself?" In a few days, you will see that *you* should have written it.

Consider the sobering results of a study reported widely in the media: Those who are the most confident generally have the least reason to be.

#10
"I give up. I'll never be any good."

Can't argue with that. If you give up, you won't be any good. Or at least you won't get any better. The idea is to stay with it. The idea is that writing is a life-long learning process. Remember that: process. The thing you write, the essay, the magazines story, the book, the script, is the product. What gets you there is the process. If you don't enjoy the challenge of its frustrations and headaches, if you can't be patient with yourself as you learn, as you hit a plateau and seem to stay there forever, if you can't stop doing these *Stupid Things*, then you should give up. But I'm betting you're made of sterner stuff. So stop reading, and get to work!

12

WHY I WRITE

See what I see, learn what I learn

Why do writers write? Do readers think about this at all? I know writers do – especially when times are tough, when an editor says no to the seventh pitch in a row, when work on the book stalls, when we are stupid enough to stop and figure what our hourly wage is. So it's not about *money*, at least not for the tens of thousands of us writers who aren't J. K. Rowling. And it's not about *fame*, at least not for the tens of thousands of us writers who aren't J. K. Rowling. (In fact, most writers do not want to be public figures. Writing is a solitary activity, and it tends to attract people who like solitude.) And it's not about *power*. (This country's powerbrokers are politicians and CEOs not wordsmiths. Dammit.)

So what is it about? Why do writers write?

In his famous essay, "Why I Write," George Orwell lists four "great motives," the first being sheer egoism, which he defines as the desire to seem clever and to be remembered after you die.

Okay, I admit it. Sometimes I lull myself to sleep thinking about how a great great great grandchild of mine will discover my name in the Library of Congress catalog. I am immortal! And I didn't even have to sell my soul or have my blood sucked.

Orwell goes on to list three other somewhat less self-aggrandizing motives, all of which I can claim as my own: aesthetic enthusiasm (the joy of working with words, of creating art out of language), historical impulse (the desire to find out what happened and preserve it for posterity), and political purpose. This last one comes close to the motto the Wobblies (Industrial Workers of the World) used above the masthead of their newspaper: *The power to transmit ideas is the power to change the world.* I love that. On good days, I even think it's true

Orwell is smart, but it takes Joan Didion to nail it. Riffing off Orwell's essay thirty years later in her own "Why I Write," she has no mercy:

"In many ways writing is the act of saying *I*, of imposing oneself upon other people, of saying *listen to me, see it my way, change your mind*. It's an aggressive, even a hostile act."

I don't like to think of what I do like that – hostile, aggressive – but Didion is right, as she almost always is. Writers *do* impose themselves on readers. That's pretty much the gig. We want to grab them, transport them from their world to ours, make them look, make them pay attention, make them see what we see. And that is a kind of aggression, and a kind of egoism, or at least it comes from a place of self-confidence.

I write for many reasons, but mostly I write because I am intensely curious about…well, about most everything…and writing funds my curiosity and gives legitimacy to my nosiness. It allows me to ask questions without being a nuisance (usually). It allows me to immerse myself in people's lives without being arrested for stalking. I can even eavesdrop. At one point early in my writing career, I thought maybe I should specialize. But I just couldn't do it. I couldn't set those boundaries. And so, during the past decade,

I've written about exotic plant smuggling and assisted suicide, about Communist spies and women's basketball players, about a whorehouse in the Mojave Desert, about my mother. About Alzheimer's. About 21st century teen girl culture. About ballet. I've tackled each one of these topics for reasons both Orwellian and Didion. But mostly, I write to learn.

The question I was asked most frequently when I went on the road for *Dancing with Rose*, my book about the world inhabited by those who have Alzheimer's, was "What did you learn?" I loved answering this question because it got to the heart of why I write, why I wrote this book in particular, why I spent four months changing adult diapers at a memory care facility, why I spent a year at my desk, laboring to craft scenes and give life to characters. I wanted – *I needed* – to learn about this disease that took my mother's life and affects more than five million Americans. And then I needed readers to see what I saw, to learn what I learned. (*I, I, I*...as Didion says.) And what did *I* see? What did *I* learn? Here are the SparkNotes:

We are more than the sum of our remembered pasts. When memory fades, when people no longer have access to their histories, they do not cease to be individuals. *Personhood* remains. People with Alzheimer's are not empty shells.

When people lose the ability to use language, as those in later stages of Alzheimer's do, they do not lose the ability to communicate. Music transcends words (this was a BIG lesson for a writer to learn). So does touch. So does, at times, a chocolate chip cookie warm from the oven.

The people who care for our elderly – mostly nickel-and-dimed, working poor women – really care. Not all of them are Mother Teresa material, but for a surprising number, these gritty, in-the-trenches, underpaid jobs are a calling.

Alzheimer's, despite everything you've read, despite all you fear, is *not* the worst way to end your life.

I write so I can learn stuff like this.

13

THE 10 SECRETS TO WRITING WELL

Really?

Are there really 10 secrets to writing well? Not likely. Search the Web for "the secret to good writing," and in less than quarter of a second you'll get "about" 517,000,000 results that range from Ernest Hemingway's tough-love approach ("There's nothing to writing. All you do is sit at a typewriter and bleed.") to Marge Piercy's marching orders ("A real writer is one who really writes.")

Maybe there is only one secret: Write. And keep writing. Or is that two? Surely there is more specific helpful advice. Here it is:

Secret #1
Read

"If you don't have time to read, you don't have the time to write." Stephen King wrote that, and you'll get no argument from me.

Reading is not just a way to find out about the world, or yourself; it is an immersion in language. Whether you read a microbiology textbook or a murder mystery, a science blog or a sci-fi story, you are swimming in words, awash in sentences, carried along by a stream of paragraphs. Whether you know it or not, you are learning language along with whatever else you are reading. You are learning vocabulary and syntax, words and how they are put together. You are learning how language flows (or doesn't).

The lessons can be positive and obvious, as when you marvel at a passage that transports you to another time or place, or when, mid-paragraph, you feel in the grip of ideas or emotions. That's a writer forging a connection with words, and it's a lesson you take with you, consciously or not. The more you read, the more you have these experiences, and the more embedded the beauty and the precision of language become.

Of course, the lessons can be negative as well – the book that puts you to sleep, the story you don't scroll down to finish reading. You are learning something here too: You are learning what doesn't work, how not to put words together, how not to tell a story.

Imagine wanting to be a musician and not listening to music. That's as odd and wrongheaded as aspiring to be a writer and not reading.

Secret #2
Have Something to Say

That sounds too obvious, doesn't it? But how many times have you sat in front of a screen, mind numb, unable to write a single intelligent sentence? You tell yourself you have writer's block. You don't have writer's block. You are more likely suffering from a dearth of material, a paucity of ideas – the lack of something to say. Perhaps you haven't worked your ideas through in your head. You aren't clear about what you think. Or maybe you haven't done the necessary research. You don't know your subject well enough yet. You can't write well if you are not in command of the material.

A great writer is smarter than his or her material. A great writer writes from a place of knowing. Simply put: You can't write well if you don't know what you want to say.

Consider how all of us, at times, are reduced to babbling. Sometimes our lips seem to be moving faster than our brains. Words come out. We sputter, stop and start, ramble, backtrack, circumlocute. The lips keep moving, but there is little sense and less meaning behind the words because we haven't stopped to figure out what we want to say. Friends may indulge us, but readers don't.

It's hard to lose a reader if you're tweeting 140 characters. But if you don't have something to say – and you're not Beyoncé, Bieber or the Pope – you're not going to snare, and keep, many followers.

Secret #3
Organize Your Thoughts

Without a plan, writing well is much more difficult than it needs to be. It is not, however, impossible. You can write without a plan if you want to rewrite and revise and restructure many times over. But it is much more sensible, more efficient, and decidedly less stressful to think about how you will structure the piece – whatever its purpose or platform – before you begin writing. Some forms of writing have their own internal structure and provide a kind of template you can use. But even if the template is provided, you need to organize your thoughts and your material within it. And so, determined to write well, you sit with the material, review everything, think, scribble notes to yourself, consider missing details, think it through, think again. You don't rush to write. You take the time to understand the material. From that understanding can come good ideas about how to structure the piece.

You would think this might be useful advice for longer pieces only. How much planning and structuring are necessary, after all, to write a 300-word blog post? As an active blogger for almost five years, I will tell you: A lot. It is harder to write short than long. There's a famous quote about this, at various times and in various places attributed to Benjamin Franklin, Henry David Thoreau, Mark Twain, George Bernard Shaw, Voltaire, Pascal, Winston Churchill, Woodrow Wilson and Bill Clinton: "If I had more time, I would have written a shorter letter." (Pascal, a French mathematician, inventor and writer, said it first.) What he – and all who repeated it later – meant is that writing short involves planning, focusing, organizing and editing. The fewer words you have to work with, the more intensive (and time consuming) the process.

Secret #4
Consider Your Audience

Unlike the instant messages, texts, or updates meant for friends, professional writing is meant for public consumption. But what public? How can you write well if you don't know who will be reading? You can't – or at the very least you stack the deck against it. If you don't know or can't imagine the audience, you are not sure how to approach these folks, what level of vocabulary to employ, what tone to choose, how to structure what you want to say. Should you use humor? Is word play appropriate? Will irony work? Who knows – if you don't know your audience.

That's why companies fund market research: to see who is out there and how best to reach them. That's why magazines conduct readership studies or run surveys to gauge what their readers think about certain issues. That's why serious bloggers track their readers using various diagnostic tools. That's why Facebook knows more about you than your mother. Knowing the audience is a key to good writing.

Secret #5

Know Grammatical Conventions and How to Use Them

Ah, the fundamentals. Note that knowing grammar becomes important only when you have something to say, have figured out how you're going to say it, and know to whom you're talking. The rules themselves – memorizing verb forms or knowing when to use a comma – don't exist without a context. The context is writing. You learn the rules for one reason: to play the game. And knowing the rules allows you to play with them, stretch them and break them (when appropriate, for effect). Breaking a rule on purpose can be creative, artful and entertaining. There is, however, a word for breaking a rule you didn't even know existed, and it is "error."

Writing well means making countless good decisions, from choosing just the right word (see #6) to crafting phrases and clauses and sentences and paragraphs that say just what you want them to say, with precision, clarity, and grace (see #7). This lofty but achievable goal is possible only if you understand the architecture of language and the building blocks of prose, only if you are at ease with the tools of the trade. Imagine a carpenter who can't use a skill saw, a dancer who doesn't know the steps, a programmer who can't write code. That's a writer without a command of grammar.

Secret #6

Master a Solid Working Vocabulary

Sculptors have clay; painters have paint; writers have words. It's as simple as that. Writers have to figure out how to connect with an audience – spur thought, evoke emotion, pose questions, entertain, tell a story, set a scene, make a character come alive –

and all they have are words. Happily, words are some of the most potent tools around, perhaps the most potent. (Remember the saying "The pen is mightier than the sword"?) Words carry not only meaning but shades of meaning. What variety, what nuance, what tone! Look up "talk" in a thesaurus and you will find "chatter," "mutter," "mumble," "gossip" and "schmooze," each with its own connotation, each with its own feel. And words not only have meaning and nuance but also sound and rhythm.

Building a good vocabulary means reading widely. It means both appreciating the smorgasbord that is the English language and learning to use words with proper respect. It means choosing the correct word, the word that means exactly what you mean, and spelling it correctly. Building a vocabulary does not mean seeking out multisyllabic tongue twisters or collecting fancy or elaborate expressions. It means being able to use words like "chatter," "mutter," "mumble," "gossip," and "schmooze" when called for.

Secret #7
Focus on Precision and Clarity

If you think clear, crisp writing just flows naturally from fingertips to screen, you couldn't be more wrong. Good writing (even bad writing) doesn't just happen. Regardless of comments like "the story just wrote itself," believe me, stories do not write themselves. Writing with precision and clarity – saying exactly what you mean, no fuzziness, no confusion, no second or third reading necessary – is hard, purposeful work. But it's work your readers expect you to do. If you don't, they are a click away from forgetting you ever existed.

Clear, powerful writing is the result of good decisions, from choosing the right word to crafting just the right construction, to relentlessly slashing clutter from your prose. Redundancies? Euphemisms? Jargon? These are obstacles to precision. Misplaced modifiers? Split constructions? Run-on sentences? These are the enemies of clarity. Yes, seemingly simple grammatical decisions make an enormous difference.

Secret #8

Hear Language

"Write for the ear," scriptwriters, podcasters and broadcasters are told, but this is good advice for all writers. It doesn't matter whether the audience actually hears aloud the words you write or just "hears" your prose when reading silently. In either case, readers attend to the sound and feel the beat. If you can master the skill of writing for the ear, you are one step closer to writing well.

Listen to the words you use. What meaning is conveyed by their sound? Listen to how words sound together. Do they fight one another? Do they flow? Say your written sentences out loud. Do they have a rhythm? A long sentence can lilt. A short sentence can tap out a staccato beat. Purposeful repetition of words or phrases can add rhythm, as can the emphatic use of parallel structure. Experimenting with (and eventually mastering) the aural nuances and subtleties of language is one of the joys of writing.

Secret #9

Revise

Think you're finished once you write it down? Think all you have to do is a quick once-over, a spell check, and it's out the door? Most writing, from stories to scripts, blog posts to books, demand much more than that. They demand revision. Having the patience and fortitude – and humility – to really revise is what separates the amateurs from the professionals. Revision is much more than tidying up, pruning, and polishing prose. It is an opportunity to see whether the writing works. It is a chance to rethink what you are trying to say. Consider the word "revision": "re-vision" means to look again, to look with new eyes. This is what the revision process should be.

And so thoughtful writers, determined to produce clear, powerful, even memorable prose, take a deep breath after they have "finished" whatever it is they were writing. Now it is time to look at the piece and ask: Does it say what I intended it to say? Have I established the mood, the tone, the voice I want for this piece? Have I written enough or too much? Taking revision seriously means asking the tough questions and being prepared to spend the extra time to answer them.

Even with the best intentions, it is very difficult to learn the art of revision on your own work. You know what you mean even if you don't write what you mean. Thus, when you read your own work, you read what you know you meant and not necessarily what you have written. A talented and patient editor can help you see what you have and have not accomplished. If you are lucky enough to find one, be attentive, be humble, and sponge up all you can.

Secret #10
Apply the Seat of the Pants to the Seat of the Chair

The final secret to writing well is the easiest to state and the hardest to accomplish: Put in the time. Just like mastering a musical instrument or a new sport, learning to write takes practice – lots of practice. This means time – good, concentrated, focused time over weeks and months and, yes, even years. Some people have a natural facility with words (probably because they are voracious readers). Others struggle. But everyone who wants to write well, talent notwithstanding, has to work hard at it. It is easy to get discouraged. It is easy to get distracted. It is *very* easy to get distracted. Multi-tasking and writing are wildly incompatible. Writing as a uni-tasker is hard enough.

14

ATTENTION MUST BE PAID

Let's hear it for uni-tasking

I was watching my son work the other night. He was lounging in the big chair in the living room with his Macbook on his lap working on the design of a new website for me. He had his earbuds in and was listening to White Stripes. He was also talking to me. He was also, in between design ideas, alternately checking Google News and playing *Call of Duty*. My daughter, sprawled on the couch, was reading *Catcher in the Rye* while listening to Bon Jovi on her iPod and watching an episode of *Glee* on TV.

Everyone is media multi-tasking these days. And multi-taskers are much admired. How rich and exciting their lives are, so chockful of stimuli! How technologically sophisticated! Cutting edge! And how, well, *efficient*. I mean, imagine how long it would take to first read a chapter of a book, *then* listen to an entire CD, and *then* watch a TV show. The mind boggles. Actually, the mind toggles – but I'll get to that in a moment.

In my non-writing hours, I too am a media multi-tasker. I just came back from a trip into town, for example, during which, in addition to driving, I listened to a Van Morrison CD, spoke on the phone (semi-legally via Bluetooth) applied Burt's Bees lip balm, caught a few minutes of *All Things Considered* and, with one hand on the wheel and one eye on the road, jotted a note to myself about all the things I was doing (almost) simultaneously so that I could come home and write this sentence. Aren't you glad you weren't on the road at the same time I was?

Most of us can agree that automotive multi-tasking is hazardous to our health – the multi-tasker's, her passengers', other drivers', not to mention the wildlife. I would like to suggest – well, more than suggest, emphatically declare – that media (or any other kind of) multi-tasking is dangerous the intellectual and creative health of the writer.

You may be one of those millions who've become accustomed to media overload in your everyday life. It works for you. But, sad to be the one to break the news: *It really doesn't.* Decades of research have shown that the more tasks multitaskers attempt, the worse they do at them. A study reported in the *Proceedings of the National Academy of Sciences* found that heavy multitaskers were more easily distracted by irrelevant information than those who weren't constantly in a multimedia frenzy. And a Stanford university study of more than 250 college undergrads (that is: veteran, skilled, uber-multi-taskers) found that the more media multitaskers used, the poorer their performance. Memory, ability to focus, and ability to switch between tasks all suffered – mightily.

In fact, brain research shows that there is no such thing as multitasking. The brain cannot do two tasks simultaneously, unless one is what researchers call a "highly practiced skill." That means – not to worry – you *can* walk and chew gum at the same time. But the brain cannot simultaneously perform tasks that require focus, like writing, reading or carrying on a conversation. Instead, a kind of toggle mechanism (told you we'd get back to toggle) allows the brain to switch from one activity to another. You may think you are talking to a friend and checking out a Web site simultaneously, but your brain is really switching rapidly between one activity and another.

The reality is that when you try to perform two or more related tasks, either at the same time or alternating quickly between them, you not only make far more errors than you would if you concentrated on each task individually, but you actually take far longer (as much as double the time) to complete the jobs than if you had focused on each in sequence. Multitasking is not a time saver; it's a time waster.

And it is an energy diffuser. Writing is tough. When we do it – if we want to do it well – we have to give ourselves up to it. *Focus on focusing* as a friend wrote in her status update, which I just checked right after I ordered those Moroccan spices online and immediately after I wrote "Writing is tough."

So, apparently, is walking the talk.

15

LABOR OR LEISURE?

You can never tell when a writer is working

What is work to a writer? This is not a question we'd ask if we were contemplating the daily efforts of a plumber or a sales clerk, a barista or a lawyer, a carpenter, a nurse, or a bus driver. That work is visible and self-evident.   It happens in front of us, straightforward, understandable. The plumber unclogs a drain. The clerk rings up a sale. The barista pulls a shot.

But what of the writer?

Thumb-tacked to a shelf above my computer, in my writing room, is a file card on which I have scrawled a quote from Wallace Stevens. Stevens was a successful New York lawyer and a big-time insurance company executive before he began the much harder work of becoming a Pulitzer prize-winning poet.

Here's the line:

"It is not always easy to tell the difference between thinking and looking out the window."

Writing *is* thinking, or thinking made manifest; thoughts ordered, set down, crafted, honed, and polished. So what Stevens is really saying, or what he is saying to me, every day, many times a day, when I look up at this quote is: *It is not easy to tell when a writer is working.* Whew. That's a relief. Because if you were here right now watching me work, this is what you'd see:

Me looking out the window.

After a long minute that stretches into several, I get up and refill my water bottle. Then, perched on the inflatable ball I sit on rather than an office chair, I bounce up and down. I look out the window. Bounce. Drink water. Look.

Then, finally: I type words on my keyboard that appear on the screen. I delete. I type. I delete. I type. You can hear the click click of fingers on keys. You can see that I'm doing something, so that means I'm doing something. This is the *real* work of the writer, right?

Wrong. The real work is the looking out the window. That's when I think, when ideas come (or not), when structure forms (or crumbles), when connections happen (or don't). It may look as if I'm doing nothing – daydreaming, goldbricking, lollygagging – but most of the time spent gazing out over the weedy meadow I can see from my office window, I've got quite a few neurons firing. Most of the time, I'm on the clock.

But it's not just the line between writing and reverie that is blurry when you're in the word biz. It is also the line between work and play, between labor and leisure. A few mornings ago, I was swimming laps with a friend of mine, an historian working on a book. After three-quarters of an hour of vigorous freestyle, we pulled ourselves out of the pool and sat on the edge, panting. "I figured it out!" she said to me, pulling off her cap and grinning. "I figured out how to make that transition work." While she was swimming, she was working.

That happens to me too. Regularly. Sometime during those endless laps, after my mind quiets, after I stop worrying about my daughter's grade in science, after I stop planning dinner, after I stop obsessing about what the chlorine is doing to my hair, ideas come to me, solutions to problems appear. Some of my clearest thoughts, my sharpest insights come when I'm not trying – when I'm "playing."

And what about all the hard work I am doing when it looks to others as if I'm just curled up with a good book? Reading is a pleasure, a hobby, a form of entertainment, so I must be "at play." But I am also at work. I am immersing myself in language, hearing the sounds of words, swaying to the rhythm of sentences, learning how writers reveal characters, how they tell stories.

In the name of work, I have done many things others would consider play: going to the movies, taking a train ride from Los Angeles to Seattle, touring one of the finest botanical gardens in the country, spa-hopping across northern Tuscany. I've flown in a vintage airplane. I've watched a season of college basketball from a seat right behind the players' bench.

But I have also done some actual, bona fide, sweaty labor in the service of my writing. For my book, *Dancing with Rose: Finding Life in the Land of Alzheimer's*, I took a bottom-of-the-rung, minimum-wage job as an aide at an Alzheimer's care facility. There, for more than four months, I cared for a dozen people who could not care for themselves. I showered them, brushed their teeth, toileted them, changed their diapers, hefted them from bed to wheelchair to couch. I cut up their food, fed them, did their laundry. It was a tough job. And that was the easy part.

The hard part was the hours, days, weeks, and months of searching for and finding the right words to tell their story, to make those experiences come alive. The hard part was being still. The hard part was looking out the window.

16

WASTING TIME

Sometimes life is just life, not plot

We're back from a three-week, 7,500-mile trek across America, my two sons and I. It has been one of those Experiences with a capital E, traversing the country on the diagonal, northwest to southeast and back, in a 24-foot rented RV. My sons are 13 and 11, old enough to be decent company but young enough still to listen to me, at least some of the time. We saw what we planned to see: national parks, Civil War battlefields, historic settlements, the Mississippi, the Gulf, the Atlantic, their Orlando grandfather. But that's not what made the trip an Experience.

What made the trip an Experience was catching a glimpse of a pale green Luna moth with an eight-inch wingspan one night in Checotah, Oklahoma. Or pulling into a gas station in Ogalalla, Nebraska, just ahead of a pick-up truck with an eight-foot statue of Elvis bungeed in the back. Or the humid, buggy night we camped at Eskew's Landing, "Mississippi's Best Kept Secret," a 200-acre former plantation. "There's been an Eskew on this land since 1859," the old woman drawled from behind the counter.

I was there, but I came close to missing it. I was almost too busy being a writer.

For the first few days, as we barreled across Oregon, Idaho, Utah, and Arizona, my mind worked overtime turning every observation into a story. My reporter's notebook was on the floor next to me, wedged between the driver's seat and a shoebox full of triple-A maps. It couldn't be any closer unless it was on my lap.

Our second morning out, my older son fell asleep riding shotgun, and I sneaked a glance at him: the long legs, the lanky arms, the feet that were suddenly two sizes larger than mine. By next summer he would have a deep voice. By next summer he would be giving me that sulky how-can-I-possibly-be-related-to-someone-as-lame-as-you look. I was sure there was an essay in this. I grabbed for my notebook, balanced it on the steering wheel and scribbled ideas as we sped across southern Idaho.

Morning three, we drove through heavy fog west of Chicken Creek Reservation in central Utah. The weather looked ominous – gray and cold and stormy – and I prepared myself for hours of tough driving. But the front I imagined turned out to be only a fog bank, and we were through it and back in sunshine in less than five minutes. I was so buoyed by this, by having something turn out so much better than I expected, that I wanted immediately to write about it: Hail the pessimist who goes through life pleasantly surprised; pity the optimist who can only be disappointed. I grabbed the notebook.

Day four, I filled pages with seventy-mile-an-hour scrawls. I was drowning in ideas: "Everyone ought to love the place they live," read one entry. I wrote it after watching a girl on horseback gallop across a field next to the highway. The land was baked brown and hard and dotted with scrub, unlovely and, I imagined, unloved. But the girl, her long, chestnut hair streaming behind her, had a huge grin on her face. *She* loved it.

Next page I wrote: "RV subculture – class collision," which came from pulling into a KOA campground the night before and finding that our assigned space was between a $250,000 motorcoach featuring a washer and dryer, and 50-inch television – and a 1962 Airstream held together by duct tape.

On day five, negotiating hairpin turns in Zion National Park, I was struck with an idea for another essay. I went for the notebook but realized I couldn't write and keep us on the road at the same time. "Zane," I called to my younger son, who had the best penmanship, "come up front and help me with something." I handed him the notebook and started dictating.

We inched around another switchback, the one-lane road snaking between towering cliffs the color of terra cotta. I kept talking, glancing over at Zane to make sure he was getting it all.

Then, *I* got it: There he was, head buried in a notebook dutifully recording my words in his careful cursive so I could later make a tale out of a moment neither of us was living. Later that day, when we stopped for gas, I took the notebook from its place by my seat and put it in an overhead storage cupboard next to a six-pack of SpaghettiOs.

Plato said "a life which is unexamined is not worth living." But I don't think he meant examining should take the place of living. I don't think he meant we should be so busy mining our adventures for meaning that we don't have time to live them.

Of course writers use their lives as text and context. That's part of the gig. Everything I have written in the past decade and a half is deeply connected to my life, a reflection of who I am or who I was or what mattered most. I know that life and art can mix, enriching both. But the danger – the danger I recognized when I saw my son hunched over a notebook instead of marveling at the landscape – is that art can overpower life. It can, for a long moment, actually replace the experience of living.

I recently met a woman whose mother had just died of cancer. She might have spent the last year of her mother's life with her mother, but instead she chose to spend it hundreds of miles away at the keyboard, crafting long, lyrical, literary letters about her mother's illness which she arranged to send to an acquaintance. Before she drafted the first letter, she imagined the book the letters would some day become.

She told me this proudly while on tour promoting the book, and I tried hard not to look horrified. I appreciate that writing can be therapeutic. No doubt the letters helped her through a difficult time. But writing also detached her from the present – from *being present* – and shielded her from the moment. Her present was painful, mine was pleasant, but we were both prisoners of our craft.

I was at first concerned, scared really, that I'd be wasting the experience of the trip if I didn't write about it. But I am beginning to understand that it pays to "waste" some things, if wasting means living the moment fully rather than taking notes on it for later.

We've been home for a while now, but I still cherish the long mid-June days I wasted with my sons, the mornings full of talk and silence, me driving, the boys taking their turns sitting up front by my side, sometimes dreamy, wordless, other times deep in monologues full of mind-numbing details about computer games and wars waged with little pewter action figures. But there was thoughtful talk too, conversations about what makes a good friend and how you decide what you want to be when you grow up and why grandma died.

At noon we would stop at some local park, where the boys would explore the terrain and play tag and fight off the insects while I busied myself in the tiny kitchen heating up cans of Chef Boyardee ravioli and slicing apples. I loved to watch them from the window and listen to their voices, loud and confident. Wherever we were – Little America, Wyoming; Cape Girardeau, Missouri; Byhallyah, Alabama – they were immediately at home. The afternoon stretched out before us. We would eat and then spread the maps on the grass and plot the rest of the day: how many miles, how many states, which campground.

After lunch, they would often disappear into the upper bunk for hours to drowse or read or play with their Gameboys or get on each other's nerves. I drove in silence, aware of them jostling above me, happy to be close but separate. Some afternoons Zane would sit by my side, and we'd listen and relisten to a tape of *Wind in the Willows*, enjoying the tale of Rat and Mole as if we hadn't heard it a dozen times before, looking over and smiling at each other at the same silly bits of dialogue we always did. Other afternoons it would be Jackson, my older son, who would join me. Sometimes we talked. Once we whiled away an afternoon composing an epic poem about road-kill. But often we simply sat together, our minds blanked by the tedium of the road. We listened to the thrumm of tires on pavement. We breathed the warm, close air. Time slowed.

There was real pleasure in this boredom, these hours and days and weeks of traveling together, of being together, of just being. The things we did, the places we saw, the thoughts we had about ourselves and each other were part of that time, and that time alone.

I think some adventures should be lived just for the sake of the adventure. Some feelings should be private; some lessons learned for one's benefit alone. Life, even for a writer, can just be life, not a narrative to be crafted and sold.

We leave for a camping trip to the mountains next week. The reporter's notebook stays at home.

17

ALL HAIL THE MENTOR

Or not

She is kind and sympathetic, knowledgeable and wise. When you tell her your story was rejected, she tells you about the twenty-three rejections she once got and how she locked herself in the bathroom and cried and then burned the letters one by one in a fine, cleansing ritual. When you hit a brick wall trying to get through to an editor, she suggests an alternate path. When you're frazzled, struggling to balance your writing life with the rest of your life, she tells you about the daily juggling act she performs. She – or he – is your is mentor, your counselor, your guide, performing the same function that the goddess Athena, assuming the mortal form of the first recorded mentor (whose name *was* Mentor), performed for the wandering Odysseus and his son.

We hear a lot about mentors these days, about formal mentorship programs at schools and places of work, about the art of "mentoring." But what exactly is a mentor, and what can you expect from the relationship? As it is unlikely that Athena will meet you at the local Starbucks to offer advice over skinny lattes, where can you find your own mentor? And do you really need one?

Should you instead consider being your own wise counselor?

A mentor is someone who has been where you're going, who has met the challenges you see ahead for yourself, someone whose work – and perhaps life – you want to learn from or perhaps even emulate. Both role model and trusted adviser, a mentor can offer a sympathetic ear and a critical eye, a shoulder to cry on and, if need be, a swift kick in the rear. Less chummy than a friendship, less formal than the tie between employee and boss, more personal than a student-teacher relationship, the connection between mentor and protégé can last a lifetime.

Experience sometimes – although not always – brings insight and wisdom, and if you can avail yourself of that through a mentor, you may be the better for it. Certainly conferring with a more experienced writer enlarges the scope (albeit vicariously) of your own experience. The relationship can be empowering and inspiring. It is, if nothing else, heartening to know someone who has succeeded in ways you would like to succeed.

But mentors are not – with the exception of Athena – godlike. They can only do so much. A mentor can share potentially useful war stories, help you network, put things in perspective, give you pep talks and offer insider tips. If you want career and life advice or suggestions on how to deal with professional and craft concerns, a mentor may be able to help. But you shouldn't expect a mentor to teach you technique (take a class for that) or read and edit your work (join a writers' group). You shouldn't expect a mentor to get you published or hired or promoted. You shouldn't expect a mentor to solve your problems. A mentor is not your Mom or your Dad, your agent, your psychoanalyst, your guru, or your personal savior.

A good mentor is hard to find, and it is not difficult to understand why. After all, the person you would most like to have as your mentor is a busy and successful writer, just the kind of person who already has far too much to do without making time for you. He or she has gotten this far by focusing energy, by selfishly guarding writing time. You are asking for this writer's most valuable asset: his or her time. And you are proposing what in many ways is a one-way relationship, with the mentor on the giving end and you on the receiving. Given all this, why would anyone agree to be your mentor?

In fact, some people do sign on. Their reasons can be altruistic or egocentric or, realistically, a bit of both. For many mentors, there is a satisfaction in lending a helping hand, in making use of their generally hard-won experience to smooth the path for one who follows. There is emotional or psychological recompense for playing a potentially important role in someone else's life. For others, being admired is the motivating factor. Who wouldn't want a kind of literary side-kick hanging on one's every word? Still others come to the relationship with a need to control and dominate, a Pygmalion-like desire to mold a person in their own image.

Whatever the case, seeking a mentor takes time and initiative – and, even with a major expenditure of both, may still not end in success. Where and how you search depends on where you live and your access to other writers and people in the literary world. One obvious place to look is the classroom. A teacher or a workshop, seminar or conference leader may be mentor material. Not all teachers are mentors. They are too busy being teachers (and most likely writers on the side, or vice versa). But, speaking as a writer/ teacher myself, I find it hard to resist that occasional student who absolutely shines, who cares more than anyone else, who surprises me – and, *this is important*, who is relatively low maintenance. And so, even though I really don't have time, I find myself mentoring a few special people. The lesson here is that when you take a class or attend a writing workshop, think not only of what you will learn during those days or weeks but also of setting the stage for a long-term relationship with the teacher.

Local writers can also be tapped as mentors. If you don't know any, start canvassing your community. Quiz your local bookseller about who writes and lives in town. Go to book-signings, attend library or literary guild readings, go to events sponsored by writers' groups. There you can make initial contact with writers who may be in a position to mentor you.

On the other hand, you can be mentored by someone you've never met – in cyberspace or elsewhere – and who is totally unaware that he or she is playing that part in your life. For years I was mentored by Joan Didion and John McPhee, neither of whom knows I exist. But I learned and took encouragement from their work. I scoured interviews and reviews for hints about their working lives. I call that being mentored. What might you learn from afar by adopting a writer as your secret mentor?

On the *other* other hand, not everyone needs or wants a mentor. If you see yourself as a pathbreaker or a pioneer, if you are particularly stubborn and strong-willed (and I mean that in the best way), you are undoubtedly committed to making it on your own. There is something to this business of "learning it the hard way." A mentor might save you the grief, but in doing so, might also short-change your experience, stunt your growth, or make you into a clone. The self-confidence you get by going it alone may be well worth the extra struggle. And, in the end, you may learn more – about your craft and yourself – than you would if someone had held your hand along the way.

Can you be your own mentor? Most definitely, yes. But this means much more than "getting in touch with your inner mentor." It means taking control of your writing life. It means learning how to buck yourself up when you need to, give yourself stern lectures when warranted, take responsibility for both your failures and your successes and trust, deep down, that you know better than anyone else where you're headed.

18

CROSSING GENRES

Fiction and nonfiction writers have a lot to teach each other

There's fact, and then there's fiction, right? There's work that's a product of careful research, and then there's work that's a product of the imagination. Nonfiction looks outward for verification. Fiction looks inward for truth.

It's a simple dichotomy. Too simple. The more I read, the more I write, the less sure I am about this distinction.

Take, for example, a nonfiction book like *Dutch*, the Ronald Reagan biography, in which the author invented characters and inserted them into the historical narrative. Or consider Geraldine Brooks' extraordinary novel, *Year of Wonders*, which is so thoroughly fact-based that to call it fiction is to deny its authenticity.

This seemingly porous membrane between nonfiction and fiction makes for interesting reading and spirited coffeehouse discussion. But does it mean anything to us writers? You bet it does. It speaks to the possibilities of crossing genres – of nonfiction writers taking a stab at fiction, and vice versa. Genre-crossing can spur a fresh way of looking at material. It can widen creative horizons, present new challenges, and expand publishing opportunities. And what's so weird about it anyway? If it's writing we love – the thrill of finding and crafting a story, the art of putting words together to create images and tap into emotions – then it's *writing* we love, not "magazine feature" writing or "short story" writing.

Sometimes, it seems, the material itself tells you to cross over. I don't mean this in some mystical, my-characters-speak-to-me, muse-on-the-shoulder way. Fiction writers might come across a true story that's so good, so powerful, so appealing that they'd be nuts to turn it into fiction. The material just screams nonfiction. Or a nonfiction writer researching a true story finds it's impossible to tell it as nonfiction. There may be privacy issues that prevent the use of sensitive material. Or there may be discrepancies or contradictions that can't be resolved and stand in the way of a strong narrative.

I know, I know. It may seem presumptuous – and it most certainly seems terrifying – to cross over. Isn't there some secret the other folks (the ones who write in the genre you don't) know?

Maybe not.

Although fiction and nonfiction writers craft different literary products, they use the same tools. Language is the most basic and important of these. It's the writer's Swiss Army knife – the tool that can be used to create everything from lyric poetry to advertising jingles. Language crafts the scaffolding of a story through perfect words, felicitous phrases, graceful sentences, seamless transitions, and powerful paragraphs. Do it in one genre, we can do it in another.

And fiction and nonfiction writers also share a highly developed sense of story. They know – through reading, through writing, through living, by intuition – what makes a good story. One story may be a product of the imagination, another the product of reporting, but the skill in identifying the story is the same.

Writers in both genres also pay close attention to the people who populate their stories. Fiction and nonfiction writers understand the importance of characters to the narrative and use similar methods to make these people come alive on the page. Description, judicious inclusion of backstory, and an understanding of motivation all feed into the construction of character. The skill's the same, whether the outcome is fiction or non. If you know how to construct a character, you know how to construct a character.

The same goes for conversation. Nonfiction writers are alert to the good quote. They know it when they hear it, and they know just when to use it in a story. For fiction writers, the skill is used in the construction of dialogue. In either case, it's the attuned ear of the writer listening for the words that best reveal character, advance the story, and keep the reader immersed.

That said, we have our strong suits, and we can learn from each other.

Here's what fiction writers know: They know how to construct scenes. They know how to weave description, narration, and exposition into prose that makes a moment come alive. They know how to place the reader in the moment with sensory details and cinematic sweep. They know about pacing. They know when a story ought to move quickly, when to spin out a long scene or zip by and summarize. And they know how to construct endings. They understand that a reader needs to leave a story feeling satisfied. It's not that a lesson must be learned or that all loose ends must be tied. But stories have to end purposely.

And here's what nonfiction writers bring to the table: They have a powerful combination of curiosity about the world, attention to what's capturing the public's imagination, a notion of what might soon be important, and a sense of obligation to write about it. It's the talent for looking outward for material, of immersing oneself in life and discovering issues, themes and people worth writing about. They look up from their navels. They look beyond what they already know, the life they've lived. And they are keen observers, careful listeners, and strong researchers.

I am infuriated by nonfiction writers who play fast and loose with the genre. And I am mystified by fiction writers who exploit real and true stories, changing just enough to call it fiction, and just enough to disrespect the story. But I love that we can all learn from each other. And should.

19

UNLEARNING LESSONS

The long road from news to narrative

Some years ago I undertook the laborious task of unlearning the most egregious of the journalistic lessons I learned during my four expensive years at Medill School of Journalism. Given that I didn't pay that much attention in class – I was too busy knocking on the doors of perception (and you Huxley fans will get that) – I was surprised to discover that I'd internalized enough to make the transition from news writer to storyteller a long and challenging one.

I had to unlearn, among other things, what a story was and how to write it. I had to unlearn how to interview. I had to unlearn what it meant to revise. I had to unlearn voicelessness. I had to unlearn arrogance. As it turned out, most of the important lessons I had to unlearn had to do with people.

I had been taught in journalism classes to think of people in very specific ways. People were either objects in a story or they were sources of information in a story. If they were objects, things happened to them (they were robbed; they won the lottery) or they did things (gave a speech, voted for a bill, hit a home run). If they were sources of information, you mined them for usable material. Either way, what you did with people was this: You asked them questions. They answered. You scribbled. If you were lucky, you got a good quote. Maybe, if you were looking for "color," and if your editor didn't expect the story in thirty minutes, you actually posed these questions in person. And, in between scribbling the answers to the questions, you looked around for descriptive details to insert in the story (if your editor hadn't warned you that you had only seven inches). "Cluttered desk," you wrote down diligently. "Coffee stain on tie."

But most times, you never saw the people who were either the objects or the sources in your story. Email had not been invented back then (although we did have indoor toilets), but had it been, a news writer trained as I was would certainly have used it extensively. And so there would have been a good chance you would not even hear the voices of the people in your story, be able to pick up any hesitation, any excitement or boredom, hiccoughs, regional accents, whatever. But really, it didn't matter if you saw a person or heard a person, or how little you knew a person, because people only existed to tell you things or to answer your specific questions so you could tell things about them.

This attitude toward people and their place not just in a story as written but in the process of thinking about and developing a story was the biggest thing I had to unlearn, my biggest barrier to being the kind of writer I wanted to be. I started unlearning on the very first journalism job I landed after graduation. I remember, during this brief and undistinguished stint as a reporter, doing a story about de-institutionalized mental patients (this was California) who were writing poetry and painting as a way of dealing with their psychoses. I actually met several of them, read their work, saw their paintings, asked the questions, got the good quotes, wrote the story. A few weeks after the story was published in the crappy little newspaper I worked for, one of the women I'd interviewed, the one I quoted most, committed suicide.

I was dumbstruck. I had spent forty-five minutes with her, a journalistic eternity. She had answered all my carefully crafted questions. I was sure I understood her, sure of how I had portrayed her in the story: She was a survivor. She was going to make it. Not only that, she was helping others make it. What happened? How could I have been so wrong? Maybe, I thought to myself, I hadn't listened too well. Or maybe I had asked the wrong questions.

In fact, what I had done was to ask the questions that were important to me, looking for the answers I needed for a story I was already constructing in my head on the way over to see her. When we met, I set the tone. I framed the discussion. I decided what mattered. At the time, I didn't see this as arrogance. It was just how I was taught to do the job. Her suicide forced me to reconsider.

I had come to her with questions, but how did I know what was important to *her*, what mattered to *her*? Suppose I had come with no questions and just let her talk. Suppose I had listened not just for the quotable quote but for clues to understanding her. I didn't. I did the interview. I shook her hand and left. And I missed something big. I don't mean the suicide. I think I could have missed the suicide even if I had been this woman's best friend for years, or her therapist What I missed was seeing her as a character, an actor in her own life – not an object in my story.

I wish I could say that from that moment on my attitude changed toward the people I wrote about. But it didn't. Not right away. Like all important lessons, this one had to be learned and relearned. The lesson that finally stuck came when I was writing my first serious work of narrative nonfiction, *Stubborn Twig*. The book was a chronicle of three generations in the life of a particular family, the Yasuis. My idea was to make history intimate through the 20th century experiences of this family, to use the Yasuis to tell a quintessential American story: the penniless immigrant who makes good in the New World. I spent more than two years getting to know the family before I started to write. This time I was not imposing myself on the material. Because I held myself back from directing the conversation, I was able to learn from this family. In fact, I was not a writer as much as I was a student. The Yasuis were not sources; they were my teachers. They knew; I didn't. That dynamic opened up their world to me.

During that time, something else happened. Homer and Miyuke Yasui became more than characters in the book I was writing, they became friends. We ate dinner together. We exchanged Christmas gifts. Miyuke taught my oldest son origami. She gave me her secret recipe for "World's Best Cookies." (They are.) Maia Yasui opened her home to me. Holly Yasui let me into her life. The line between writer and subject blurred. A barrier came down. My Medill teachers would have been horrified.

I, on the other hand, was thrilled. I felt I had finally arrived at a way of interacting with people that felt neither superficial nor exploitive. When I granted the Yasuis the power to teach me, lead me, direct me, tell me what was important to them rather than what was important to me, when they befriended me and vice versa, I crossed over into a new way of writing. Here people were their own unique selves, actors in their own dramas that, if you stayed and watched long enough, if you were quiet and curious and attentive enough, you might just catch a glimpse of.

20

WRITE LIKE ME

Is style measurable?

A few days ago my husband alerted me to a website that promised to reveal what famous writer's writing my own prose most resembles. My husband had tried it, pasting in several paragraphs of a chapter of his most recent book, *The Alchemy of Air*, and the site had informed him that he wrote like H. G. Wells. He was pleased. My husband is a science writer. Next he tried a passage from another of his books, *Demon Under the Microscope*, and the analysis came back: Margaret Mitchell.

I was, when I got his email about this site, in the midst of writing yet another freebie – a post for a high-traffic blog that may or may not help with the promotion of my book, *My Teenage Werewolf* – so, of course, I immediately stopped what I was doing and logged onto the site. (I'll give you the URL later…providing yet another reason for you to read through to the end.) I pasted in a passage from the book, clicked "analyze," closed my eyes and began to pray, mumbling *Joan Didion Joan Didion Joan Didion* under my breath. When I opened my eyes, here's what I saw: James

Foster Wallace.

At first, I drew a blank. John Foster Dulles? No, he was a Secretary of State, wasn't he? Charles Foster Kane? Nope. That was the Orson Welles character in *Citizen Kane*. Then, I remembered: James Foster Wallace, the guy who wrote those enormous novels that some readers and reviewers revered (*Time* included one of his books in its All-Time 100 Greatest Novels list) – and most people struggled to finish. The guy they called a "hysterical realist" and compared to that other guy who wrote enormous novels that some readers and reviewers revered – and most people couldn't finish: Thomas Pynchon. The guy who offed himself. Great.

The revelation that my prose resembled Mr. Wallace's did not cause me to go out and buy one of his books. But it did cause me to think, for the godzillionth time, about the writer's Holy Grail: Voice. Or Style. Or whatever you want to call that distinctive something that makes your prose uniquely yours. What is it, that I-know-it-when-I-read-it thing, anyway? And have I labored lo these many years to develop whatever it is only to discover that some other guy – albeit deceased – already has dibs on it?

As I was angsting about this – which was a much more engrossing activity than doing the freebie writing I was supposed to be doing – my husband came in and informed me that he'd posted the who-do-you-write-like site on facebook, and that two people we both knew had already tested out their prose. One was a twenty-something recently graduated physics major. I had no idea he wrote anything, let alone long passages of prose. The other was a veteran writer, Evelyn Sharenov, whose work I had published in an online magazine I edited. Both pasted in their prose, clicked "analyze," and received the news that their writing resembled...James Foster Wallace.

I don't know what sort of algorithm the creator of the site

concocted to analyze prose passages. Truthfully, I don't even know what an algorithm is. Or why it's not spelled algo*rhythm.* Maybe the only three writers he calculated in were James Foster Wallace, H. G. Wells and Margaret Mitchell. Maybe Joan Didion wasn't even a choice. Maybe – not maybe, *certainly* – this was all a silly and meaningless exercise. It was high time for me to stop worrying about my writing sounding like someone else's and get back to actually, well, writing. And so I did.

But I would like to say just a few words about voice (or style). About how, in some technical way, it might have to do with the length of a sentence, or the number of sentences in a paragraph, or the average number of syllables in words used, or some other countable attribute (numbers of commas? percentage of text in dialog?). But that really voice is immeasurable. It is the product of a writer's way of seeing and being, the eye that underlies the I (and vice versa). It's the vision – and the original expression of that vision. For a nonfiction writer like me, the vision comes not just from who I am and how I see the world but also from the kinds of stories that attract me (because of who I am) and the kinds of questions I ask when pursuing those stories (because of how I see the world). My voice or style or whatever it is comes from the originality (on a good day) and quirkiness (pretty much every day) of my take on the world, the unique nature of my immersion in the material, and then, of course, the words I find to express all that.

I don't think iwl.me is going to offer much insight into that process. Yep, there it is, the site. Go there, paste in a few paragraphs of your work, and see what happens. I'd like to know how many James Foster Wallaces there are out there.

21

I HEART BLOGGING

The joy of going commando

Two years, two blogs and 166 posts ago, I wrote an essay, conceived in crankiness and dedicated to the proposition that bloggers and writers were not created equal.

I am no longer the "reluctant blogger" I called myself back then, but I am still cranky, and I still believe that producing content for a blog often has as much to do with writing as making a box of Kraft Mac 'n' Cheese has to do with cooking. The metastatic blogosphere – there are now more English-language blogs than there are people in the U.S. – does include some winners: the occasional smart political or current events blog, the high-cred/ high-geek science and technology blog, the you-must-have-this-*now* cool gadget blog, the blog you have to love because it feeds some idiosyncratic hobby (fire hooping?) that your real-life, 3-D friends make fun of and don't want to hear you talk about and, of course, the oh-so-discerning blog that features interviews with you or reviews your book (just saying).

And it also includes blogs written by people who know how

to think and write. Let's call these folks "writers." I am a writer...who blogs. Kind of like a woman who runs with wolves but without the wolves. Since I last wrote about blogging, I have, despite myself, come to appreciate its place in my creative life. To conceive, write, and publish a little essay about whatever I think is important or noteworthy or funny, is a luxury. I think it's a luxury I've earned. Compare blogging to the process of getting an essay published in what I charmingly still refer to as the "real" media. Three months ago, I pitched a national magazine, suggesting three essay topics. A month later, I got a return email, which began back-and-forth correspondence, which resulted in an assignment. (The process could just as well have resulted in no assignment, which for most writers pitching national magazines is the norm.)

So I wrote the piece. I wrote it carefully and thoughtfully, the way I try to write everything that appears under my name. It has ever-so-slowly made it's way up the editorial chain of command, been edited thrice (along with my own revisions and tweaks) and is scheduled for publication five months from now. So, from idea to publication: close to nine months. A woman could grow a baby in this length of time. I could – and will have – conceived, written and published more than 40 to 50 blog posts in this time. Of course, the blogs I give away. The magazine work I actually get paid for. But being in control of your own work is a welcome change. Liberating, even. Fun. I greatly respect good editors (and have luckily encountered a few of them in my writing life) and would not want to go commando all the time. But some of the time...hell, yes.

Blogging is a discipline too. I write – really write – these 300+/- word posts. I craft them, polish them, try to make them engaging and, at least occasionally, insightful. In other words, I practice the art and craft of writing. And I do this whenever I want to, without waiting for permission or contracts or assignment letters — and without remuneration, I will add again in case you missed the first reference. I now view blogging the way a performing pianist might view practice sessions. It's the discipline that keeps you nimble. It's the training that improves the art and keeps you focused. It's rehearsal for the real gig, which for me is still publishing in "real" media.

So I am no longer reluctant. But I am still cranky because most of what I see in this sphere in which I now happily and creatively publish is garbage, a digital landscape littered with ghost-written celebrity blogs, too-much-time-on-their-hands (and not enough ideas in their heads) personal blogs, blogs that dying newspapers have forced their reporters to write.

Now — just to add to the mess — there are hundreds of thousands of ersatz business blogs, a tsunami of sites manufactured (note I don't say "created") by companies that are busy trying to persuade every plumber, manicurist, and mechanic that he or she needs "an active web presence." My favorite such company is called Hat Trick Associates. These good people want to handle your "content writing" (this "writing" should not be confused with that thing writers do) because *You Need Content That Is Optimally Shared Online And SEO-Friendly To Ensure Future Visitors And Revenue.*

Oh. I thought I needed content that was interesting, engaging, and well written. Silly me. I cannot resist telling you that the company's motto is:

We. Create. Content.

I would offer this alternate motto:

We. Don't. Know. Punctuation.

Probably I can relax about all this because blogs may soon be a legacy medium, with the action moving over entirely to social networking sites, mobile apps and whatever other technology has been invented since I started writing this piece two hours ago.

22

MEMORY, FACT AND TRUTH

Whose truth should you tell?

My brother has a sharply detailed memory of falling off the stage at the rec hall at summer camp when he was seven: how he couldn't stop crying, how the counselor sent another boy over to the girls' camp to get me, how I ran in, panting and sweaty and sat down on the wooden floor with him on my lap, and hugged him and rocked him until he stopped crying.

It was an extraordinarily important moment for him, he told me recently. He was scared that summer. It was his first summer at sleep-away camp, eight weeks away from Mom and Dad living in a cabin with strangers. He had been homesick and lonely. But that day when he fell and I came running was, he said, a turning point for him. Realizing that his big sister was just a shout away made all the difference.

I was 15 that summer, and I remember those eight weeks at Camp Tamarac with crystal clarity. It was the summer I won the Taconic Invitational Girls Tennis Tournament. It was the summer that the boy I had a crush on for the previous two summers finally paid attention to me. We kissed a lot that summer. He gave me his ring, which I wore on a chain around my neck. It was silver and had a large onyx stone. A few weeks later, he broke up with me. I remember the heather blue crewneck sweater I wore to the dance the night he dumped me. I remember the song that was playing. I remember he smelled of Canoe cologne. Although that summer happened more than three decades ago, I still remember the names of every girl in my cabin. I could draw you a schematic of the cabin, which girls slept in which cots.

But I don't remember comforting my brother in the rec hall. Truth be told, I don't remember my brother even *being* at summer camp that year. I have no memory of him whatsoever. He is part of no incident, no scene, no conversation I can remember from that summer.

Did this incident happen? My brother is sure it did. Me? I just don't know. Whose version of the past is the right one? If you were interviewing my brother and me, what story would you write about that summer?

Let me tell you another story about memory, fact, and truth.

My husband, a science writer, wrote a biography of Linus Pauling, one of the greatest scientists of the 20th century. During the course of the research, my husband interviewed Pauling many times. The man had a prodigious memory, the kind of memory you would expect a genius scientist to have. He was at the end of his life then. He was in his 90s, but time and time again what Pauling told my husband was corroborated by other people, by letters and papers and documents, by the work of other historians. His recall was amazing.

One of the anecdotes Linus Pauling told my husband was this:

When Linus was about seven years old, he and his cousin were caught by a workman while exploring a half-finished building. This was in Condon, Oregon. Linus tried to wiggle out the window, but the workman caught him by his pants, dragged him back inside and beat him with a piece of lath. Linus ran home sobbing. He tearfully told his story to his father, Herman, who listened carefully, then led his son by the hand through the streets of Condon in search of the workman. They found the fellow, Pauling remembered, eating lunch in the crowded dining room of the town's biggest hotel. Herman asked him if he had beaten his son. When the man answered yes, Linus recalled, Herman knocked the fellow to the floor – and was subsequently arrested and tried for assault.

Pauling's recollection was just the kind of a juicy anecdote the narrative writer salivates over. It was vivid and specific and meaningful. It was also...wrong. When my husband checked the police records to get additional details about the incident, he discovered that Pauling's father was, indeed, arrested and put on trial in Condon during the year that Linus was seven. But he was arrested and tried not for assault – there was no record at all about the assault – but for bootlegging whiskey during a time of local prohibition. (He was acquitted.)

What story would you write of that incident?

Here's what my husband did He recounted, in vivid detail, the anecdote as told by Pauling. He then presented the documentary evidence that disproved Pauling's story. He didn't do that to show that Pauling had a faulty memory or to show off what a meticulous research he himself was. He did it because Pauling's erroneous story illuminated something about him – which, after all, is the purpose of biography. After recounting the anecdote and the reality of the Pauling's father's arrest, he added this sentence, at the end: "His son's fond mixing of memories reveals his image of his father as a sympathetic protector who suffered because of loyalty to his son."

In other words, although the story Linus told was not true in the sense of being factual, it was emotionally true. But not just that: In its flawed factuality, the anecdote revealed a bigger truth than the event itself. It revealed how Linus perceived his father at the time and how he needed to remember him. That perception is tremendously important. The story Pauling told becomes even more important, more potent, when you find out it wasn't factually true.

So really we are talking about two kinds of truths: factual truth and emotional truth. As narrative nonfiction writers, should we care about both? About either? About neither? Which truth, whose truth should we tell?

This is not an easy question to answer. It is maybe more difficult today than ever before, as factual truth has taken a beating – from Random House to the White House.

We live at a time when Reality TV is scripted and edited and everybody knows it, and it is still called *Reality*.

We live at a time when nonfiction, the label, the title, is suspect. When something is published as nonfiction – that is, *fact, reality* – that is not the end of the conversation but the beginning.

These days we have the infamous but certainly not singularly culpable James Frey, who wrote a nonfiction book which turned out to be, in some important aspects, fabrication. We have a Holocaust memoir that is almost entirely fiction. We have an acclaimed memoir written by an edgy teen which is later discovered to be the concoction of two middle-aged writers – not just the book itself but the author, the persona is a complete fabrication. What are we to make of this?

Have we gotten to a point where there no difference between truth and fiction?

I am here to say there *is* a difference. And, as a true believer in the power and authenticity of nonfiction, I am here to fight for that difference.

This is not to say that in fiction, in everything from pure fabrication to misremembered events, there cannot be great truth...great *emotional* truth. Of course there can be.

But I think the responsibility of nonfiction writers, as tellers of other people's stories, is to find and verify the factual truth while appreciating, honoring, and learning from the emotional truth. We *enhance* the emotional truth when we pay attention to the factual truth. We do not have to sacrifice factual truth for emotional resonance, just as we do not have to sacrifice factual truth for dramatic storytelling.

No sacrifices are necessary. We can have both factual and emotional truth, both factual truth and dramatic storytelling. It takes work. It takes diligence. But it is work we must do.

Here are ten guidelines for the narrative nonfiction writer:

1. Remember that we are in the nonfiction business. *And proud of it.*
2. Recognize that there is factual, literal truth – that may or may not be independently verifiable – and emotional truth.
3. Remember that factual truth does not have to be, nor should it be, sacrificed in favor of emotional truth.
4. Recognize that factual truth – or lack thereof – enhances emotional truth. Knowing that the story Linus Pauling told about his father is not true makes it even more poignant than if it were true. If my husband had just accepted and told this story as literal truth, he would not only have been remiss in his duty to nonfiction, but he would have ended up writing a passage that had *less* power than it does.
5. Determine what is verifiable and make an effort to verify. Names, dates, places, descriptions can often be checked in documents and reports, press clippings, reference books,

maps, scrapbooks, photo albums.

6. Listen carefully and openly to divergent stories, different tales told of the same event by different participants. Don't disregard conflicting information. The conflict itself is interesting to the story.

7. Find the factual truth if you can.

8. Understand the emotional truth that lies beneath it...either beneath the literal truth or, if the story turns out not to check out, the emotional truth underneath the falsely remembered story.

9. Balance the two for a story that has both authenticity and resonance.

10. Do your part, with every story you write, to hold the line. Readers need to get back a sense of confidence that what is presented as nonfiction *is* nonfiction.

23

RE-THINKING THE INTERVIEW

Is there a worse way to get to know someone? I think not.

I was midway through recounting a humorous, character-revealing personal story – just the sort of juicy anecdotal material interviewers lust for – when the guy interviewing me interrupted my story to ask what I considered a trivial, oddly off-point question. Being a veteran interviewer myself, I stopped to consider the error of his ways, the *many* ways that what he had just done was wrong.

For starters, he interrupted me mid-sentence. There really is no worse behavior for the interviewer, particularly when you've got your subject warmed up enough to tell a story. But interrupting was only the symptom of a much larger problem. If there is a cardinal sin in the world of interviewing, it is not listening. He interrupted because he wasn't listening. I also considered the question he asked, some factoid that had no relevance to the point I was making with the story. I thought about the nature of his question and how it revealed more than his lack of listening. It revealed how his mind worked. Which was not how mine worked. He asked a question that was important to him, not me. And, not for the first time, I considered how this journalistic practice of asking questions – that is, choosing what questions to ask and in what order, when to follow up, when to let it go – often says more about the interviewer than the interviewee.

And so it seems to me that we've got a problem.

We've got a much-used, much-beloved, downright enshrined method of gathering information and stories that is severely, maybe fatally, flawed. In selecting questions, we journalists direct the conversation. We ask what we think is important – which may or may not be what our interview subject thinks is important. Or has thought about at all. The questions we ask are a product of who we are and how we think. But don't we want to know who the person we are interviewing is and how that person thinks?

I would like to suggest the heretical: Interviewing is a lousy way to get to know someone you want to write about. It is a planned, staged, ritualized encounter that exists outside the real and ongoing life of the interview subject. The "conversation" that is presumably taking place – those who write about interviewing always use the word "conversation" – is not a conversation at all. It is not a back-and-forth exchange of ideas and stories. It is orchestrated, directed, and channeled by one of the participants, the journalist, who has an agenda. No, I don't mean an evil, hidden agenda (although sometimes that may be true). I mean a plan. The plan is: Collect information and anecdotes, opinions and ideas for the purpose of crafting a particular kind of story of a particular length for a particular audience. Alternately, it may be orchestrated by the interview subject, who has an agenda: Looking smart, creating a platform, furthering a position, promoting a cause, etc.

I'm not suggesting that interviewing never works, that there are no good interviews or smart interviewers. In fact, there have been a handful of astonishingly talented and insightful practitioners of the journalist interview: Bill Moyers and Oriana Fallaci come to mind (and Stephen Colbert was brilliant too). But as a journalist who has interviewed hundreds of people and as a writer who has herself been interviewed scores of times, I am not a big believer in the process.

In this staged "conversation," one person – the interview subject – is expected to spill the beans, whatever those beans might be, while the other person – the interviewer – remains comfortably opaque and detached. *Tell me everything while I tell you nothing* is the operative plan. *Trust me* (because I say so) *with your story. I'll decide what's important. I'll pick and choose from what you say in response to my questions. I will then disappear with the material and craft the story. You can find out what I did with the material you entrusted me with when everyone else in the world finds out, when it's published or posted.*

Interviewing is not only a lopsided non-conversation that is a poor way to get to know someone well enough to write about him or her. It can also be a dangerous (and lazy) way of gathering facts for a story. It's not so much that people lie about facts when you ask them – some do, most don't – it's that they don't know or they misremember. If you want stats, read the report. Don't ask the person who read the report (among dozens of others) last week. Or even the person who helped write the report, which may have gone through so many edits and revisions that the person can no longer remember what made the final cut. If you want facts and figures, dates, statistics, do the work to ferret out the most credible, best documented source. This is usually not a person.

Interviewing – if interviewing means asking questions to get responses – does have a function, albeit limited: If you want a quick opinion about something you deem important, a quote or a sound bite to fit into a story, then ask the appropriate person.

Otherwise, I would suggest that journalists consider more authentic, more thoughtful ways of delving into the personality and the peccadilloes, the motivations and challenges, the beliefs, attitudes, quirks (you name it) of a person important to the story they are crafting.

I would suggest that journalists consider adopting the methods and mind sets of oral historians and cultural anthropologists. Like oral historians, journalists should pose open-ended prompts that invite the respondent to frame and self-direct the response. They should not ask narrow, specific questions that come from the journalists' sense of what is important. And, like oral historians, they should listen.

L I S T E N. Listening does not mean keeping your mouth shut while someone else is talking. It means attending to what is being said. It means quieting your own mind and being present in the moment, finding an intensity of focus that allows you to absorb what someone else is saying. Journalists ought to try it more often.

And, like cultural anthropologists who want to learn about people and places, about how others live and the choices they make, journalists should consider the fine art of observation. Yes, watching. Active, vigilant, thoughtful, keen-eyed watching. Ask yourself this: When is a person more likely to reveal something about his or her character – sitting across from a journalist in a staged interview answering journalist-directed questions or when out doing what he or she usually does, when participating in his or her own life, when corralling children or leading a meeting, pumping iron or playing *WoW*? Someone once said that the very best way to assess a person's character is to see how the person treats his or her dog.

Observation is the challenging act of putting oneself in the right place at what could be the right time. And waiting. It is the active cultivation of curiosity. It is both knowing what to look for and being absolutely open to seeing the unforeseen. It is, as with active listening, about being quietly, intently alert, like an animal in the forest.

Here's something else you might want to consider about interviewing: Although journalists may love interviewing – it gets them out of the office; it is easy and quick (compared to deep research, active listening and focused observation); it can perk up a story with quotes or sound bites – many people actually *hate* being interviewed. I know. I asked them.

Top Ten Reasons People Hate to be Interviewed

1. Journalists are ill-prepared. They haven't done their homework. It's annoying and insulting.
2. The questions they ask are boring and predictable.
3. The questions they ask are invasive and insensitive.
4. Journalists don't listen. They can't wait for you to stop talking so they can ask the next question.
5. Journalists have their own agenda. They're not actually interested in you. They're interested in some story they've already half-created in their heads.
6. Journalists operate on their own schedule. They want to meet when and where it's convenient for them.
7. Email interviews are the worst. Journalists fire 15 different questions at you. It takes hours to answer all of them.
8. Broadcast interviews are the worst. Journalists don't realize how uncomfortable the camera makes most people.
9. Journalists take my words out of context.
10. Journalists always seem to choose the quotes or the clips that make me look and sound the stupidest.

11. Bonus: Journalists always promise to send links or clips or at least tell you when the story is going to run. They don't.

So there you have it. Although my crowd-sourced survey was decidedly unscientific, I think the results are very much worth considering. They speak to flaws in the interviewing process, most of which are within the journalist's control. (Note that I argue the basic *premise* of interviewing is flawed and that we ought to look at smarter more thoughtful ways of interacting with people we want to learn about.)

Two things that struck me about the responses I received: First, they were immediate. Fifty-six people responded *within the first hour* of my posting the prompt: "Tell me about your experiences being interviewed by a journalist." Wow. Obviously this is a hot button for some people. Second, many of the respondents were downright angry. They lashed out at journalists using much harsher language than I included in the Top Ten list.

That's something to think about. Hard. When the go-to journalistic method of gathering material from and about people causes this kind of reaction, when it exhibits as many deep flaws as it does, it may be time to rethink the method.

24

THE ART OF THE GUINEA PIG

Welcome to in-the-trenches research

When did I first realize what I had gotten myself into?

Was it that morning in the 102-degree Bikram studio when, slick with sweat, leaving little puddles on my mat as I grunted through a series of yoga poses, I face-planted during a strenuous downward dog sequence and gave myself a bloody nose?

Maybe it was the evening of the twelfth day of my detox and fasting regimen when I made chicken parmesan and spaghettini for my family and then sat down to a sludgy gray rice protein shake.

Or it could have been that afternoon at the Bowerman Sports Clinic, cycling hard on a stationary bike with a heart monitor strapped to my chest, a pair of plastic clips pinching my nose, a mask-and-hose contraption crowning my head, and a nervous young grad student inexpertly pricking my finger every three minutes.

At some moment – really at *all* these moments and more – I thought to myself: This whole human guinea pig approach to researching a book has its, uh, downside. Why exactly am I doing this again? Why aren't I sitting comfortably at home in my nice, book-lined office? Or ensconced in a whisper-quiet archive? Or off interviewing someone, preferably in an exotic locale? Why am I sweating, bleeding, gasping for breath, downing Maca-infused wheatgrass shots (don't ask), and otherwise making my life unpleasant? *On purpose. And for a year.*

I had to keep reminding myself why. And so I'd take a deep breath and turn up the volume on the self-talk: *You're on a quest. You're on a journey. This is an adventure.* It was true: I had set out to investigate the world of anti-aging, a weird world that was an almost seamless blend of fantasy and reality, of science and hucksterism, of life-changing research and unadulterated opportunism. I wanted to separate the hope from the hype – and take my readers along for the ride. How I'd decided to do that was to not only look at the best research and the worst scams, to go conferences and clinics, spend time in cutting-edge laboratories and big-promise websites, to observe and questions, but also to use myself – within reason – as a human guinea pig.

I had vowed to try a long list of activities, as well as treatments, therapies – and ways of thinking – that held the promise of slowing or reversing aging. Could I turn back the hands of my own biological clock? Could I go counterclockwise during this year-long adventure? This was a journalistic quest – the subject fascinated me as a reporter and writer – but it was also, to state the obvious, a personal quest. I mean: *Tick tock.* The noise gets louder, more insistent (scarier) as the years fly by. I wanted to muffle that noise, slow the ticking, maybe, for a while, halt the movement of those hands. I was not interested in being or recapturing my younger self (an aimless, angst-ridden smoker with a dud of a boyfriend and a job I hated). I was interested in recapturing and preserving all those good things we associate with youthfulness: health, vitality, limitless energy, a sense of adventure.

I wanted to look good – of course – but more important I wanted to feel good, from the inside out. And so, I coupled careful research with the guinea pig approach.

[*Time out for an educational aside*:] Guinea pigs have played a very important role in medical science. In fact, their wide variety of hair types and colors made them a prime choice for studies of genetics and heredity in the 19th and 20th centuries. But it was 1890 that was truly the Year of the G. Pig. That's when the antitoxin for diphtheria was discovered using these little guys in the research lab, resulting in the saving of millions of children's lives (including many of us) and a Nobel Prize – the first in medicine – for its discoverer. Today guinea pigs are more likely to be pets (my daughter used to have a pair that she named Joey and Chandler) or menu items (a delicacy in Andean Peru, sometimes baked whole, like a suckling pig, with a hot pepper in its mouth). In case you wanted to know, mice are now the most common research lab animal (75 percent of all experimental animals) followed by zebrafish (18 percent), rats (5 percent) – and then everything else (2 percent). I have no idea why guinea pigs are still used as a metaphor for any subject of biological experimentation. But I'm sort of glad. Suppose, to be accurate, I had to tell you that I took the "mouse" approach or that I became a "human mouse" for this book. It just doesn't have a ring to it. [*End of educational aside.*]

I will admit that the guinea pig approach had its high points. During my year of research and experimentation I discovered the Face Aging Group, a loose consortium of University of North Carolina-Wilmington computer scientists, mathematicians, statisticians, and anthropologists. Together they were teaching computers how to age images of faces. Their techniques were aimed at catching years-at-large criminals or helping locate long-lost children, but they were using the science of craniofacial morphology (the structure and form of the head and face) and building on a sophisticated understanding of the principles and processes of aging. And if their computers could age a face, then their computers could also de-age a face. My face, for example.

I flew to North Carolina and hung out with them. They were a fascinating bunch, a quirky cast of characters that made me think I was on the set of *Criminal Minds*. Of course I interviewed them. Of course I read their research papers and observed their work. But the best part was when, as guinea pig, I agreed to join their million-plus database of faces. They took a photograph of my face and let the computer have at it. I sat there, astonished, enthralled, aghast (take your pick) as I watched my face age, by increments of five years, to 75, an experience that is not for the faint of heart. Then, like magic, the computer reversed the process, and I watched as my 75-year-old face lost its lines and furrows and wrinkles, as the effects of gravity slowly disappeared, as my lips plumped and my jaw firmed, and I became a version of my 20-year-old self. That was a good day.

But a month later I was lying on a hospital bed with the left leg of my sweat pants rolled up to expose my upper thigh while an exercise physiologist prepped, draped, swabbed, and anesthetized the "sample site." Then, while he chatted about his research, he dug around in my thigh for two perfect samples. It was quite the thing to see little chunks of your muscle meat on a piece of sterile gauze, let me tell you. It was times like these when *you're on a quest/ you're on journey/ this is an adventure* just didn't cut it. It's times like these I had to say: Hey, *this'll make a good story*.

I hope it did.

25

LIVING A LIE

What would you do to get a story?

"Writers are always selling somebody out." Joan Didion said that.

"Every reporter is a kind of confidence man, preying on people's vanity, ignorance or loneliness, gaining their trust, and betraying them without remorse." That's from journalist, essayist and author Janet Malcolm.

These are harsh words. Merciless, even. If they came from a choleric media critic, a sneering pundit or a nasty ideologue, they would be easy to dismiss. But they come from within the ranks of writers. In fact, they come from two of our most intelligent, most thoughtful late 20th century American nonfiction writers.

I've been thinking a lot about this indictment of journalists as casual betrayers since I finished reading the very young writer Kevin Roose's book, *The Unlikely Disciple*. In it, the 19 year old chronicles the semester he spent as a student at Liberty University, Jerry Falwell's ultra-conservative school in Lynchburg, Virginia, a place where the "intelligent design" wing of creationism is considered too liberal. Roose took a leave from Brown University, where he was in his sophomore year, to experience the world of Liberty. Living in a dorm, taking a full load of classes and participating in extracurriculars, he immersed himself in student life and culture, seeking to learn how hard-core evangelical Christians his own age think and act.

Good idea. We need hard-working, energetic reporters to help us understand "the other," to get beyond stereotypes. And immersion is the way to do it.

But immersion does not mean lying about who you are. It doesn't mean buddying up to the people around you – dorm mates, dates, well-meaning pastors – and "seducing" them, as Janet Malcolm once wincingly put it, so that you can later disappear and use their lives, their words, and their struggles in your book. The book no one knew you were writing. Because everyone thought – you *told* them – you were just a kid like them, a transfer student.

Roose got his story by misrepresenting himself and living that lie, every day, for four months, and, as an immersion reporter myself, this bothers me a lot. Mind you, I am not a purist about going undercover. I wish I were. It's an easier position to defend than the one I hold, the infamous "end justifies the means" one. If a reporter has to sneak around and lie to get a very important story, a story which, when told, will save or improve lives – a story on eldercare abuse or sweatshops, for example – then I'll make peace with hidden cameras or faked resumes, with lying to sources to get them to trust you so you can get the goods on them. It's not pretty. But, well, the end justifies the means.

But Kevin Roose was not reporting a story of such magnitude. Or, really, *any* magnitude. His findings, aside from not saving or improving lives, were not even at all surprising. He finds that his evangelical classmates are not all cut from the same cloth. While some are straight-ahead Bible-thumpers, others struggle with their faith. He finds that although – or more likely *because* – sex is verboten at Liberty, it is the most common topic of conversation among his male dorm mates. He finds that some Liberty students who publicly parade their purity have actually done the deed.

Which of these revelations would he not have gotten had he been honest about who he was and what he was doing? I wonder. As an immersion reporter myself, as someone who has explored (as an announced writer) the world of college women athletes, the world inhabited by those people who suffer from Alzheimer's and those who take care of them, and the world of teenage girls (the scariest of the three, by the way), I know what every experienced reporter knows, what maybe Kevin Roose, an inexperienced reporter, hasn't yet learned: People want and need to talk about themselves. They crave someone who will really listen, who is truly interested in who they are and what they think. They want and need to make sense of themselves, and telling their stories, even their secrets, helps them do this. Ordinary folks (non-celebs, non-politicians) open up over time. You don't have to fool them into it. You don't have to pretend to be someone you aren't.

On the contrary, the more transparent you are about who you are and what you're doing, the more they want to help you do it, the more they want to tell you how it really is for them. The more you hang around, interested and inquisitive, the real-er you are, the more they trust you with their stories.

And so I can't make peace with the fact that Kevin Roose pretended to be a good Christian boy, that he hid the fact that the only reason he enrolled at Liberty was to get material for a book. Would Liberty have admitted him had he written on his application that he was a left-leaning, secular Ivy Leaguer whose mission was to write a book? Doubtful. But that's not my point. My point is that the kids themselves would have opened up to him had he been honest about himself. My point is that the story he got did not merit the extreme strategy of misrepresentation and lying. The end did not justify the means.

I'm sorry to pick on Mr. Roose. I think he has talent, and I think he has a good heart. I found his book engaging. But journalism is in such troubled waters these days. Public belief in the importance of what we do is at perhaps at all-time low. We individual reporters, by the actions we take, by how we conduct ourselves, how we treat the people we write about, contribute greatly to how our profession is viewed and valued. Or not.

For the record, Roose was troubled by his own deception (but not nearly enough, in my opinion) and mentions his ambivalence from time to time in the narrative. Later, when he's back among his own kind and has finished his manuscript, he confesses his sin via email to the kids he lied to, befriended and wrote about. And being good Christians (and kids with not that much to lose), they forgive him.

But I suspect many of them will never think kindly of a reporter again, that their experience being hoodwinked by the author has made palpable for them the Christian Right rant about the arrogance and corruption of the godless media. And so the author has not only done a disservice to his subjects, he has – like those writers who fabricate and call their work nonfiction – weakened respect for the profession, eroded the integrity of what we do, created suspicion and distrust, made it harder for the rest of us.

26

CONJURING CHARACTERS

Why can't art imitate life?

In art as in life, some characters stay with us, vibrant, alive, resonant, remembered down to the detail. Long after we've forgotten the twists of plot or the particulars of dialog, we remember the person: Ibsen's Nora, Fitzgerald's Daisy, Willie Loman, Holden Caulfield, Frank Sinatra at 50 as captured by Gay Talese, Gary Gilmore through the eyes of Norman Mailer. How do writers *do* that? How do they imprint a character so deeply on our psyches that years after reading a story, sometimes decades after reading a story, we can conjure a character in full dress?

When writing succeeds so beautifully, it may feel like magic. It *should* feel like magic to readers. But as any writer knows, it's actually hard seat-of-the-pants to seat-of-the-chair work. Not that there aren't moments of inspiration, illumination, or revelation. But in between those moments are hours (sometimes days) of heavy lifting. The "magic" of making a character come alive on a page, of creating a character we cannot forget, is really the sum of a series of very good, very smart decisions. Those decisions start with the realization that what makes a character compelling and unforgettable   on the page is exactly what makes a person compelling and unforgettable in life.

So conjure a character from your own life, a person who has made an indelible mark. Take my fourth grade teacher, Miss Moshey. Please. Many decades have passed since this woman tried, with only modest success, to teach me the times table. I subsequently completed elementary school, middle school, high school, college, and five years of graduate education, instructed by 143 other teachers, at least 100 of whom I cannot remember by name and almost as many I wouldn't recognize if they knocked on my door.

But I remember Miss Moshey. I remember her because of the physical – and to my ten-year-old eyes idiosyncratic – detail that for me defined her. She had biceps. She had lean, muscular arms that she showed off proudly, in all weather, in sleeveless dresses. I was accustomed to gentle, pillowy lady teachers, the ones who sat you on their ample laps when you skinned your knee out at recess or hugged you with big, soft arms that felt like warm rising bread dough. Miss Moshey's biceps were not just a rarity in the world of female elementary school teachers, they were emblematic of her personality. She was tough. She was no-nonsense. She was not a hugger. In fact, you didn't want to be hugged by her. It would hurt.

The other reason I remember Miss Moshey is because at the end of fourth grade she told the class that she was spending three weeks of her summer vacation on the back of a mule trekking through the Grand Canyon. That was the most exotic thing I had ever heard of. It was also the first time I considered that teachers had a life outside the classroom.

And so Miss Moshey remains a discernible, memorable character for me not because I can recall the color of her eyes or how tall she was or what she said about verbs agreeing with nouns. She's not memorable because I remember a catalog of descriptive traits or a storybook full of tales but rather because *one* revealing descriptive trait and *one* meaningful anecdote stand out.

It's worth thinking about that when attempting to make a character – real or imagined – come alive on the page. In life, and maybe in art too, less is often more. One sharply observed detail can carry more weight than a litany of lesser descriptors. One well-told anecdote may tell it all; one well-crafted scene may be all we need; one snippet of dialog may reveal all that needs to be revealed.

Writers in the act of crafting characters have many choices to make, and they must choose well consistently. It might seem at first that these choices are almost limitless. A writer could select any one (or two or three) of hundreds of different physical traits to help readers visualize a character, for example. Although the material to draw from may be at times overwhelming, in fact, writers have just a handful of ways to make a character come alive. They can write about what the character *looks like*, what the character *says*, what the character *thinks*, and how the character *acts*. Writers may also interweave backstory or use environment to reveal character, but these techniques are often tied to the basic four.

So it's not magic. It's a series of choices. It's attention to detail. It's noticing the biceps or, in the case of an imaginary character, inventing the one memorable detail – Harry Potter's lightning bolt scar, for example.

It's scrutinizing all the material – in the case of nonfiction, all the scenes observed, all the dialog overhead, all the action recorded – and using what you already know about life, about the people who remain real and vibrant to you, to make literary choices. I think it takes the terror out of making these choices to think about it this way. It doesn't make it less work, or less exacting work. It's not that talent, and a lot of it, isn't involved. It's that art can borrow nicely from life, that we can use what we know to know what to write.

27

MAKING THE PAST COME ALIVE

If you didn't see it, can you write about it?

A Communist spy sweats it out in a Brooklyn hotel room. Is the FBI on to her? Is the KGB secretly plotting her liquidation? Is the guy she's sleeping with a counterintelligence agent? She takes another drink to calm her nerves and considers her next move.

He is a small, slight man in a trim, dark suit and a Chaplinesque derby. He has the serene, unlined face of a teenager, with clear coppery skin, full lips and a high, broad forehead. Behind wire-rimmed glasses, his eyes are dark, intense, serious, like student intent on passing an exam. He is twenty-one years old, an immigrant from Japan, and he is stepping off the train in Hood River, Oregon, and looking, for the first time, at the strange landscape he hopes to call home.

Elvie goes from bad to worse. She is no longer able to eat or drink anything. She is choking on her own saliva. She is wide-eyed. Her body is stiff and tense. She knows there's a process going on, she knows she is dying, and she is fighting it. Her family is with her now, her son, her daughter-in-law, two grandchildren, and one great grandchild. They take turns sitting with her. Someone is always there. They talk softly to her. They hold her hand, stroke her arm, fluff her pillows, keep her lips moist, apply cool compresses to her forehead, rub her body with lotion.

The first scene took place in 1945, the second in 1908 and the third, just last week. They are all historical re-creations, the beginnings of nonfiction narratives I crafted from deep research rather than direct observation. The first is the opening scene of my book, *Clever Girl*. The second comes from an early chapter in *Stubborn Twig*, another of my books. The third is an end-of-life essay I'm working on right now. For each, the challenge was the same: making a moment come alive for readers, making characters real on the page, telling a compelling story – a factual not an imagined story – when I had not been there to watch, to take notes, to ask questions.

I consider historical re-creation one of the essential skills in writing literary nonfiction. Of course it's essential when writing history itself, which many narrative nonfiction writers do – from Melissa Fay Greene's story of the Springhill Mine Disaster (*Last Man Out*) to Erik Larson's chronicle of the hurricane that devastated Galveston, Texas, in 1900 (*Isaac's Storm*) to Mark Kurlansky's kaleidoscopic tale of the only rocks we eat (*Salt*).

Without the ability to re-create scenes, to animate characters, to use factual documents to craft real life, a writer is left writing a dry chronicle of events that reads suspiciously like one of those tomes we all carried back and forth in our book bags and never opened unless we had to. If you've read the books I just mentioned, you know they are anything but dry. In fact, they are page-turners.

But what about those who do not write history? Why should they learn the art of historical re-creation? First, I would argue that there is no such thing as writing literary nonfiction without writing history. History is embedded in every story we tell. The characters who populate an unfolding-before-the-writer's-eyes story all have pasts, and those pasts often hold the key to understanding who they are, what they do and what they care about. And so we find ourselves needing to re-create a moment from a character's past – a defining moment, a turning point, a traumatic event. We weren't there to see it, but it needs to be in the story.

Places too have pasts, and writing a contemporary story about a place or a story in which place is, itself, a character, means more than just being there and experiencing the locale. It means delving into the history of that place and mining its past for insights into its present.

Second, the reality of reporting a story is that you can't be everywhere, and you can't be working all the time. That means that even if you are writing a story devoid of history (if that's possible), and even if you care nothing about the past of your characters or locale (if that's possible), you still often find yourself facing the challenge of re-creating a moment you did not directly experience. Either that, or you don't include the moment.

Several years ago I was researching a book on the experience of being a female athlete (*Full Court Press*). The basketball team I was following had early morning practices five days a week, and I dutifully rose at 5 a.m. to get there in time to stand on the sidelines, observe and take notes. I did this every day for weeks and weeks. Most days nothing much happened. Entire weeks of practice would go by without offering the glimmer of a new insight. Then, one morning, my infant daughter awoke with an ear infection, and I missed practice. It was at that practice – the first I had missed all season – that one of the starting seniors broke her hand. How could I not write about that? I had no choice but to carefully reconstruct the scene based on multiple interviews and hospital reports.

So the question is: How do you tell a story – relate an event, write a scene – which you yourself did not witness?

And the answer is: The same way as if you *did* witness it. In both cases, you write from the vivid, detailed picture you have in your head. It's how the picture gets in your head that's different.

When you are an eyewitness, the images are first-hand impressions. You try hard for accuracy by your keen observation, attentive listening, furious note-taking, and interviews both during and after the event. When writing stories about events you've not personally experienced – whether they happened yesterday or a hundred years ago – you look to documents and photographs and interviews and whatever else you can think of to build those mental images piece-by-piece.

The process of re-creation begins with knowing – or more accurately, learning over time – what it is you need to vividly write a scene, from what was for lunch that day to the color of the couch to the precise chronology of events. The detail you train yourself to notice if you are an eyewitness is the same detail you need to discover from other sources if you want to make the scene come alive.

And so the work begins. You brainstorm the kind of sources that will likely, or even possibly, get you the depth, quality, and precision of information you need. You investigate public documents and private papers. You scour newspaper accounts, court records, census data, photographs, weather service reports, oral histories, Congressional testimonies – whatever makes sense given the story you are after. You conduct interviews. You watch and listening to recordings. You read poetry. You immerse yourself in the moment you are trying to recapture.

Then, if you are diligent, patient, and resourceful, careful, thorough, and a little lucky, the pictures start forming inside your head. You see them, you focus, and you write from that place of vivid detail. Or, as often happens, you soon discover that you can't write, or can't write well, because something missing.

I spent weeks doing research to re-create a particularly dramatic moment in a character's life, one of those "let's just see what you are really made of" moments. I had hours and hours of taped conversations. I visited and revisited the locale. I pored over maps. I read newspaper accounts. I thought I had it. But when I sat down to write the scene, I discovered that I was missing one seemingly small detail: the weather.

My character was going to be walking the streets of Portland, Oregon, for hours waiting to be arrested (to test the constitutionality of a curfew for Japanese Americans), and I had no idea if he was bent over in the pelting rain, shivering with his hands clenched in his pockets, or taking a stroll on a mild spring evening. I had to find out before I could write. And, apparently, I had to start writing before I knew I had to find out.

Art really is in the detail. And, to invert the cliché: You *do* have to sweat the small stuff.

28

ALL'S WELL THAT ENDS WELL

Why endings are so hard

"It is easier to see the beginnings of things, and harder to see the ends." That's how Joan Didion begins her essay, "Goodbye to All That." She is referring to the beginnings and ends of relationships, specifically her love affair in the mid-1950s with the city of New York. But I think it's also a wise statement about writing. It is easier – if the word *easy* can be used in relation to writing – to see the beginning of a story than it is to see the end. It is easier to know when and where to start than when and where to finish. And I think it is easier (okay, not easier exactly, perhaps just more possible) to write good beginnings than it is to craft good endings.

I've thought about this a lot (mostly during those long, tortuous hours when I am wrestling with how to end a piece), and I think I understand why.

First, it's a matter of focus. All through the imagining, pondering, researching, and organizing phases of a piece of writing – everything that happens before I sit down to write – I am focused on how and where the story will begin. As I think and observe, read, listen, and ask questions, I am constantly evaluating the material I'm getting for its potential as an opener. I want to know what that first sentence will be, that opening scene, that initial snippet of dialog, that quotable quote.

That's probably because facing a pristine screen is one of the most intimidating moments I encounter in my life as a writer. So, before I make myself comfortable in front of the computer, before I open a "New Blank Document," (even the name raises my blood pressure) I want to know what will go in it.

Figuring out the beginning beforehand, crafting the sentence or scene in my head, comforts me. It momentarily quells the anxiety I feel when that blank page appears on the screen with that insistent, mean-spirited blinking cursor challenging me to start writing *now*. Knowing how a piece will begin fools me into thinking that I will know how to write the rest of the piece, and it is precisely that sense of confidence that allows me to go ahead and do so. I knew I would begin with Didion a week ago when I was thinking through this piece on my foggy morning run.

But do I know how I will end this piece? Not a clue. I haven't given it a thought. That's one good reason it will be harder to write the end once I get there.

There's something else at work too, something purely mechanical that leads not necessarily to *easier* beginnings than endings but to *better written* beginnings: the writing process. When I'm writing a piece, I write in chunks. So let's say on day one I write the initial 500 words. Day two, back at work, I read through those first 500 words (which includes, of course, the opener), and I rewrite, re-craft, polish. Then I go on to write another chunk, let's say 750 words. Day three I begin by reading the 1250 words I've already written, including the now once-edited opener. I edit it again, then move through the piece and start writing the next chunk. And so it goes, with each day beginning by reworking and polishing the opener. At the end of the process – maybe a week to write a magazine piece, several weeks to write a book chapter – I will have burnished and refined the opening paragraphs five, six perhaps a dozen times.

Now consider the ending. It is the last thing I write and so is the least edited. I will go over it, of course – nothing goes unedited – but it will not get the same daily scrutiny the opener gets. I will not come back to it again and again, reading it through, tweaking and re-tweaking it.

And sometimes I can convince myself that it is not necessary to do so. After all, the opener has to be wonderful. It's got to entice the reader into the story. So I can justify spending an inordinate amount of time and energy on those first few paragraphs. But the ending? Hey, if the reader got all the way through the piece, I'm not likely to lose that reader if the last few paragraphs don't shine quite as brightly.

There's a third reason, at least for me, that endings are both more difficult and not as well crafted as beginnings: my early training. I went to journalism school. I learned story structure from a former newspaper reporter who passed along the wisdom of the "inverted pyramid," a way of organizing material (from most important to least) that, in fact, goes against everything we know about how to tell a compelling story.

But I didn't realize that back then. Back then, I sat and listened and absorbed the inverted pyramid, one key tenet of which was that the story ended when you ran out of material important enough to include. In other words, there was no ending, no considered, crafted way to bring a story to a close. You just stopped, like a singer ending a song when she was out of breath.

I have spent the last twenty years unlearning this, among other things I was taught in journalism school, but it is a hard one to shake off. It really is tempting to just keep going through the material until you no longer have any decent material to go through, to end when you run out of steam. It is much much harder to compose a narrative that goes somewhere on purpose and arrives there with, if not a flourish, then at least a satisfying nod.

For me, the key to writing good endings is just this: conceiving of stories as *stories* – once-upon-a-time narratives that move, not collections of material, not ordered information, but stories. Stories have beginnings, middles and ends, all of which are equally as important. An ending in a real story is satisfying. It is a lesson learned, a mystery solved – or perhaps, even more intriguingly, kept alive. Whatever it is, it sharpens the focus, weaves together and makes sense of the ideas, coalesces the story. The ending matters.

I asked my 15-year-old son (who was dubbed a "wordsmith" by his eighth grade teacher) what he thought about this beginning and ending business. He said, with little hesitation, that endings were much harder to write..

"Why," I asked.

"Because at the beginning you are free to start anywhere," he told me. "But at the end, you're stuck with where you got to."

 Like right here.

29

THE MOVING FINGER...

...having writ, moves on

I was down at UPS yesterday arranging to have the final edited version of my manuscript sent back to my editor in New York.

"Another book?" the woman behind the counter asked, all smiles. She's been following my work for a while now. "You must be *so* excited!"

Actually, not.

I'm more like – deflated. Depressed, even.

When I'm excited is when I'm writing, when I'm immersed in a subject, hip-deep in the world of the book, energy focused, all cylinders firing. The excitement begins to mount somewhere around chapter four. By then I've found a way into the book. I'm warmed up. I am seeing the possibilities, and the narrative is starting to make itself visible. Around chapter four I am keenly aware of the difficulties I face, of the challenges I will encounter and have to master if the book is to be successful. But, unlike in the throes of chapter one, two and often three, I am not in a state of semi-paralysis, fearful that I am not, nor will I ever be, up to the task at hand. By chapter four I have a toe-hold. I am by then – biochemically speaking – scared enough to have a good adrenaline rush going but not so scared as to be awash in cortisol. I am alive, alert and ready for action.

More than that: I am thrilled to be so thoroughly absorbed. My life takes on a shape. There is order to my days. Order to my reading, my thinking, my conversation, even my dreaming. The book is like a planet, and I am its moon. I love the tug of that gravitational pull. I don't ever want to be released.

And then, one day, I am. One day I find myself at the UPS counter with a stack of manuscript pages. When I place the work in a big envelope and sign my name to the shipping slip, I am closing a door I am never ready to close, no matter how many times I've been through this process. When I place the work in a big envelope and send it cross-country, I am ending an intense relationship, the relationship I have had with the characters in the book (even when one of the characters is me), with the world these characters inhabit, the world I have tried hard to understand. And I am ending the lovely, insistent, book-driven rhythm of my days: the morning run when I clear my head, when *mirabile dictu*, ideas and connections sometimes come unbidden; the long hours of thinking and writing and staring out the window and making pots of tea and circling the room and forcing that tough and wonderful discipline of seat-of-the-pants to seat-of-the-chair. I love the way writing demands tunnel vision, the way it obliterates the 21st-century multi-tasker in me. On a good day, I forget time.

Flannery O'Connor once wrote that writing a novel was a "terrible experience during which the hair often falls out and the teeth decay." I choose to interpret this not as a scene from a Coen brothers' movie (or, for that matter, a Flannery O'Connor short story) but rather as a statement about the intensity of the experience, the way it transcends and makes irrelevant the mundanities of life. Yes, I know she meant it otherwise. I have read the tortured, anguished (sometimes just plain whiny) words of writers who view the act of writing as a uniquely unpleasant form of mental, emotional, and/or psychological torture. What can I say? That ain't me, babe.

"You must be so excited!" the UPS lady said to me. I smiled back and nodded pleasantly. But what I was thinking was: How will I structure my days now? Where is the rhythm to my life? What I was thinking was: I can't wait to rush home and start looking through the telescope for a new planet to circle.

30

WRITING AS A CALLING

Why we do what we do

It's not going well.

You've been staring at the screen all morning, cursing the cursor. It's that insistent blinking. The little bugger is mocking you: *hurry up, write something and make it good, buddy.* But the words won't come. The sentences are jammed inside your head. You read, re-read, re-re-read the few paragraphs you've managed to eke out. Muddy, murky, clumsy. You know it'll get better. You know you can make it better. But it's just going to take a lot of work. You settle in for the long haul.

Or:

The sun is shining, the sky a cloudless, dazzling cerulean blue. The air, soft and warm, smells of cut grass and cherry blossoms. Not that you'd know. You're sitting inside at your desk wrestling an essay into submission (or, actually *for* submission). You look out the window, longingly, then back at the screen. It's going to take the rest of this glorious afternoon to whip this thing into shape. You sigh. You settle in.

Or:

All your friends have late-model cars and gym memberships and the newest smartphones. You've got a computer almost as old as you are, a whopper of a Visa bill and a mother who wonders when you'll get yourself a career already. You shake it off, sit at your desk, open the file with the manuscript you're working on, and settle in.

Why do we do it? Why do we keep writing, day after day, year after year? What keeps us at our desks despite the literary and meteorological challenges, the rejections, the less-than-minimum-wage (if we are masochistic enough to do the math) checks that all-too-infrequently arrive in the mail?

Some – the Few, the Proud, the Severely Deluded – might stay the course because they harbor thoughts of writing as a path to fame and fortune. Someone has to be the next J.K. Rowling, don't they? Someone has to sell that film script to Hollywood's director du jour. Someone out there lands those $20,000-an-article contracts with the *New Yorker*.

Others might keep at it because (speaking of deluded) they think writing is easier than getting a "real" job. After all, isn't it just lazing around at home in your P.J.s thinking up stuff until it's time to hang out at the local Starbucks and exchange literary gossip with other folks who've spent the morning in their P.J.s at home thinking up stuff?

For most of us, there is something else, something bigger, going on.

Most of us long-suffering, seat-of-the-pants-to-the-seat-of-the-chair writers do what we do because who we are and how we see the world has made us writers. It's simple: Writing is what we do. Stories are how we process experience, how we understand ourselves and others, how we make our way in the world. We might not say it this way because it sounds a little too much like a novitiate taking vows, but we feel we have been *called* to the writing life.

Yes, writing is an art. Yes, it's a craft. And yes, it is also a business. But for those of us who stay with it and love it (even when we hate it), it is – it *has* to be – something more: It is a vocation.

A vocation is, literally, a calling, from the Latin, *vocare*, "to call." Look up the word. It means "a strong inclination to follow a particular path." Now, for comparison, check out the word "occupation." It is defined as "a person's usual work" – a dull little phrase that has the whiff of a cubicle about it. Vocation, on the other hand, has running through it the passionate subtext of obsession, the path you *have* to follow.

What exactly is a vocation, a calling, and how do you know if writing is yours? Here's what Thomas Moore, in his book *A Life at Work: The Joy of Discovering What You Were Born to Do,* has to say: "A calling is a deep sense that your very being is implicated in what you do. You feel that you fit into the scheme of things when you do this particular work." It is, he writes, work that defines you, that completes you, that gives you a sense of peace.

If that's a bit too high-minded for you, think of it this way: What are you doing when you don't wish you were doing something else? What are you doing when you forget time and place, when you are deeply in the moment, "in the zone," as athletes call it?

Me? I am in my writing room perched on the big red activity ball I use as a chair, a mug of Good Earth tea by my side, my brain (on good days) firing on all cylinders, my thoughts clearer than they are at any other time. I am – I am both happy and sad to admit – smarter and more creatively and intellectually alive sitting on that big red ball than I am anywhere or any time or any place else.

On bad days? On bad days I try to embody what Norman Mailer once said about the difference between an experienced writer and an inexperienced one. The difference, he claimed, was only one thing: the ability to work on a bad day. And so, on a bad day, I work. I slog through it. I gut it out. There is an odd pleasure in this. There would be no pleasure at all, odd or otherwise, if writing wasn't a calling. If it was merely an activity I had some talent for, an occupation that occupied me, I would have jumped ship years ago.

Writing, for those of us who heed its calling, is not just a way to make an (often skimpy) living. It is a way to make an (often rich) life. If writing is your calling, then working at it can be a path toward, excuse the Greek, *eudaimonic* well-being. A combination of *eu* ("good") and *daimon* ("inner genius or spirit"), this word has been coined to express the deep pleasure and sense of well-being one can get from striving toward excellence based on one's unique talents and potential. Aristotle considered that effort to be the noblest goal in life. Today's neuroscientists note that such self-directed striving for excellence actually activates pleasure centers in the brain.

It's good to take solace in such thoughts when the sun is shining and the birds are chirping and you're sitting in front of computer cursing the cursor on one of those days that separate the men from the boys (which is probably how Norman Mailer *really* wanted to express it). *I am not struggling, angsting or otherwise crashing and burning*, you can tell yourself. *I am in pursuit of the noblest goal in life. I am answering the call.*

The poet and novelist Marge Piercy once wrote: "A real writer is one who really writes." I love the simple rhythm of that line, and I love what it means to me: A real writer writes despite everything (cranky children, cranky editors, bad reviews, brain freeze). A real writer stays on the path. That path may or may not lead to a National Book Award or a critically reviewed chapbook – or even publication. But it's a path that calls out, loud and clear. To ignore the call, to choose occupation over vocation is to short-circuit the creative instinct, to dampen the inner spirit – and to miss out on all that *eudaimonic* bliss.

ABOUT THE AUTHOR

LAUREN KESSLER is the author of eight works of narrative nonfiction. Her books have been *Washington Post* and *Los Angeles Times* bestsellers, *Wall Street Journal* "best" selections, Pacific Northwest Book Award winners and Oregon Book Award winners.

Her journalism has appeared in the *New York Times Magazine*, *Los Angeles Times Magazine*, *O* magazine, *Ladies Home Journal*, *Prevention*, *Woman's Day*, *Utne Reader*, *The Nation*, newsweek.com and salon.com. She is a national speaker and workshop leader.

laurenkessler.com @laurenjkessler

ABOUT THE TYPE

This book was set in Garamond, a typeface designed by Claude Garamond (ca. 1505-1561), a French type designer, publisher, and punch-cutter. He is considered one of the leading type designers of all time.

Made in the USA
San Bernardino, CA
07 October 2015